# Innovative language teaching and learning at university: integrating informal learning into formal language education

Edited by Fernando Rosell-Aguilar, Tita Beaven, and Mara Fuertes Gutiérrez

Published by Research-publishing.net, a not-for-profit association
Voillans, France, info@research-publishing.net

© 2018 by Editors (collective work)
© 2018 by Authors (individual work)

**Innovative language teaching and learning at university:
integrating informal learning into formal language education**

Edited by Fernando Rosell-Aguilar, Tita Beaven, and Mara Fuertes Gutiérrez

**Rights**: This volume is published under the Attribution-NonCommercial-NoDerivatives International (CC BY-NC-ND) licence; **individual articles may have a different licence**. Under the CC BY-NC-ND licence, the volume is freely available online (https://doi.org/10.14705/rpnet.2018.22.9782490057108) for anybody to read, download, copy, and redistribute provided that the author(s), editorial team, and publisher are properly cited. Commercial use and derivative works are, however, not permitted.

**Disclaimer**: Research-publishing.net does not take any responsibility for the content of the pages written by the authors of this book. The authors have recognised that the work described was not published before, or that it was not under consideration for publication elsewhere. While the information in this book is believed to be true and accurate on the date of its going to press, neither the editorial team nor the publisher can accept any legal responsibility for any errors or omissions. The publisher makes no warranty, expressed or implied, with respect to the material contained herein. While Research-publishing.net is committed to publishing works of integrity, the words are the authors' alone.

**Trademark notice**: product or corporate names may be trademarks or registered trademarks, and are used only for identification and explanation without intent to infringe.

**Copyrighted material**: every effort has been made by the editorial team to trace copyright holders and to obtain their permission for the use of copyrighted material in this book. In the event of errors or omissions, please notify the publisher of any corrections that will need to be incorporated in future editions of this book.

Typeset by Research-publishing.net
Cover design by © Raphaël Savina (raphael@savina.net)

ISBN13: 978-2-490057-10-8 (Ebook, PDF, colour)
ISBN13: 978-2-490057-11-5 (Ebook, EPUB, colour)
ISBN13: 978-2-490057-09-2 (Paperback - Print on demand, black and white)
Print on demand technology is a high-quality, innovative and ecological printing method; with which the book is never 'out of stock' or 'out of print'.

British Library Cataloguing-in-Publication Data.
A cataloguing record for this book is available from the British Library.

**Legal deposit, UK**: British Library.
**Legal deposit, France**: Bibliothèque Nationale de France - Dépôt légal: juin 2018.

In memory of Professor Stephen Bax

# Table of contents

vii  Notes on contributors

xiii Acknowledgements

1    Integrating informal learning into formal language education: an introduction
     *Fernando Rosell-Aguilar, Tita Beaven, and Mara Fuertes Gutiérrez*

## Section 1.

### Learning collaboratively online: attitudes, motivation, and learning communities

9    Can you teach me to speak? Oral practice and anxiety in a language MOOC
     *Zsuzsanna Bárkányi*

17   Social media in L2 education: exploring on-line collaborative writing in EFL settings
     *Robert Martínez-Carrasco*

27   Busuu: how do users rate this app for language learning?
     *Miguel Ángel Saona-Vallejos*

37   'It's a shame that we haven't met earlier!': facilitating a tandem language exchange programme at Queen's University Belfast
     *Liang Wang*

## Section 2.

### Testing and evaluating language learning tools

49   ImparApp: Italian language learning with MIT's TaleBlazer mobile app
     *Tiziana Cervi-Wilson and Billy Brick*

## Table of contents

**59** LipDub: a technology-enhanced language learning project with music
*Kirsten Mericka*

**67** Video resources in a flipped language classroom: an experience of using videos to flip a Mandarin teaching module
*Zhiqiong Chen*

**79** The Better French Living Project: how to encourage linguistic, practical, and cultural year-abroad preparation outside the classroom
*Sandra Salin*

**89** Multimodal Corpus of Spanish Speech Acts: main features and potential pedagogical uses
*Marta Vacas Matos*

**99** Twitter as a formal and informal language learning tool: from potential to evidence
*Fernando Rosell-Aguilar*

# Section 3.

## The polyglot community: an interview with Richard Simcott

**109** The polyglot community: an interview with Richard Simcott, by Tita Beaven
*Tita Beaven and Richard Simcott*

**119** Author index

# Notes on contributors

## Editors

**Fernando Rosell-Aguilar** is a Senior Lecturer in Spanish and Open Media Fellow at the School of Languages and Applied Linguistics at the Open University, United Kingdom. He is also a Senior Fellow of the Higher Education Academy. He holds an MA in Online and Distance Learning from The Open University. His research focuses on online language learning, mainly the use of apps, Twitter, and podcasting as teaching and learning tools. Other research interests include the use of multimodal synchronous computer-mediated communication and task design. He previously taught Spanish at the University of Southampton and the University of Buckingham.

**Tita Beaven** is a Senior Lecturer in Spanish in the School of Languages and Applied Linguistics at The Open University. She has a Doctorate in Education in Educational Technology from The Open University and is Senior Fellow of the Higher Education Academy. Her research is in the area of innovative pedagogies and open education, in particular open educational resources and open educational practices.

**Mara Fuertes Gutiérrez** is a Lecturer in Spanish at the Open University (United Kingdom). She holds a First Class Honours in Hispanic Studies (Philology, Universidad de Valladolid, Spain) and a PhD in Spanish Linguistics (Universidad de Valladolid, 2006, Extraordinary Academic Achievement Award). Previously, she has taught Linguistics, Spanish as a Foreign Language, and Research Methods applied to Linguistics at several Spanish and British institutions, including the Instituto Cervantes in Manchester (Associate Lecturer) and Leeds Beckett University (Senior Lecturer). Her current research interests are in the field of innovative pedagogy and in linguistic theories applied to language learning and teaching. She is the leader of the Special Interest Group in Linguistic Theories in Language Learning and Teaching (School of Languages and Applied Linguistics, The Open University) and she is a member of the research group GIEL (Language Teaching Research Group), based at the University of Valencia (Spain).

Notes on contributors

# Authors

**Zsuzsanna Bárkányi** is a Lecturer in Spanish at The Open University. Previously, she worked as a Lecturer in Spanish Linguistics at Eötvös Loránd University, Budapest. Zsuzsanna holds an MA with teaching credentials in Spanish and English Language and Literature, an MA in Theoretical Linguistics, and a PhD in Spanish Linguistics. Her fields of expertise are the interface of phonetics and phonology and L2 pronunciation.

**Billy Brick** is a Languages Centre Manager and principal lecturer in the School of Humanities at Coventry University. He teaches Multimedia in Language Teaching and Learning to undergraduate students and Computer Assisted Language Learning at Masters level and has been involved with numerous JISC/HEA projects including the Coventry On-line Writing Lab (COWL) and the Humbox, an OER project for the humanities. His research interests include digital literacies, social networking sites and language learning, and mobile assisted language learning. He is currently developing a beginners' Italian language learning app, ImparApp, together with colleagues in the university's Disruptive Media Learning Lab.

**Tiziana Cervi-Wilson** is a Senior Lecturer and the coordinator for the UWLP and career and employability modules for the School of Art and Humanities at Coventry University. She is Fellow of the Higher Education Academy and a member of the CU Add+Vantage Advisory Board. She teaches all the Italian undergraduate modules at all levels at Coventry University. Tiziana is a disruptive Educator for the DMLL (Disruptive Media Learning Lab) and a member of the School of Humanities International Network (SHINe). Her research interests include digital literacies, language learning, and mobile assisted language learning. She is currently developing a beginners' Italian language learning app, ImparApp, together with colleagues in the university's Disruptive Media Learning Lab.

**Zhiqiong Chen** started working for the Language Centre of Warwick University in 2005 when the first Mandarin academic module was established. From then on, she has been teaching various academic and Lifelong Language Learning

Mandarin modules as a teaching fellow. Outside Warwick University, she also teaches Chinese online for the Open University as an associate lecturer starting 2009. Her research interests are in language teaching methodology, blended learning, and student engagement.

**Robert Martínez-Carrasco** is a visiting lecturer in the Department of Translation and Communication at Jaume I University (Spain), where he lectures in Reverse Translation and Advanced English for Translation. He received his PhD in Applied Languages and Translation from that university in 2017, with a dissertation that explored the epistemological bases of legal translation education in contemporary higher education settings. Primarily an educator and a practising translator, his research focusses on (legal) translation training, foreign language education, pedagogy, effective training, and epistemological approaches to education.

**Kirsten Mericka** is the Austrian Exchange Service Lector in German (OeAD-*Lektorin*) at the University of St Andrews, Scotland. After finishing her Bachelor Degrees in Social Anthropology and Comparative Literature, she completed a Master's Degree in German as a Foreign and Second Language, all at the University of Vienna in Austria. She currently teaches German as a foreign language in Scotland and has also taught in the US, Poland, and Brazil.

**Sandra Salin** is a Lecturer in French Language, Translation, and Interpreting at Newcastle University and teaches at all levels. She holds a Certificate in Advanced Studies in Academic Practice and became Senior Fellow of the Higher Education Academy in May 2017. Dr Salin has led and presented a number of learning and teaching projects and has acted as Year Abroad Director since 2014. Her current learning and teaching interests include independent and reflective learning and the year-abroad experience.

**Miguel Ángel Saona-Vallejos** has taught Spanish as a Foreign Language (SFL) since 1999. He is currently doing the second year (full-time) of a PhD at the University of Central Lancashire (UCLan) on "The use of social networking sites to learn Spanish as a foreign language through blended language learning".

Notes on contributors

He teaches SFL part-time at the Manchester Metropolitan University (MMU) as well as UCLan. Previously, he achieved a Master's Degree in Applied Linguistics to Teach SFL (University of Jaén, Spain).

**Richard Simcott** is a British hyperpolyglot who has been called 'one of the most multilingual people from the United Kingdom'. Besides being fluent in more than a dozen languages, Richard also has studied more than 30 others. Richard is a Languages Director at The Social Element, a company that specialises in global social media management, where he works with global brands running multilingual social media projects. He is the co-founder of the Polyglot Conference, an annual event that brings together polyglots from around the world.

**Marta Vacas Matos** holds a PhD in Hispanic Linguistics from the Autonomous University of Madrid and a MA in Spanish from the University of Texas at Austin, as well as from the University of Salamanca. She has taught in several American and Spanish universities in the US (Colby College, Emory University, and The University of Texas at Austin), and in Spain (University of Salamanca, New York University, Stanford University, Syracuse University, and Middlebury College). She currently works at IES Abroad, The State University of New York at Albany in Madrid, and UDIMA (Universidad a Distancia de Madrid).

**Liang Wang** is currently a Language Support Officer at the Language Centre, Queen's University Belfast, specialising in Chinese language programme development and intercultural awareness training. He has led the Tandem Language Exchange programme since 2015. He holds a PhD (2011) and a Master of Research (2008) in Education and Educational Technology, and an MA in Media Technology for TESOL (2003). He has interest in internet-mediated intercultural language education and intercultural communicative competence development.

## Reviewers

**Inma Alvarez** is a Programme Leader of the Doctorate in Education at the Open University. She has researched on intercultural competence in language education in relation to teacher training and learners' skills development, learning in the digital era, as well as on expression in the performing arts. She has participated in a number of national and international research projects. At present, she is a co-investigator in the AHRC-funded Language Acts and Worldmaking project.

**Zsuzsanna Bárkányi** is a Lecturer in Spanish at The Open University. Previously, she worked as a Lecturer in Spanish Linguistics at Eötvös Loránd University, Budapest. Zsuzsanna holds an MA with teaching credentials in Spanish and English Language and Literature, an MA in Theoretical Linguistics, and a PhD in Spanish Linguistics. Her fields of expertise are the interface of phonetics and phonology and L2 pronunciation.

**Anna Comas-Quinn** is a Senior Lecturer in Spanish at the School of Languages and Applied Linguistics at The Open University. Her work centres on the production and delivery of online distance language learning courses. She researches in the area of technology-enhanced learning with a focus on open education in language teaching and learning, the use of open educational resources, and the development of open pedagogical practice amongst language teachers.

**Rodrigo Hernáiz** is a Lecturer in Spanish at the Open University since 2017. Before joining the OU, he taught Spanish at the Philipps-University Marburg (Germany) and worked as an FPI researcher at the Faculty of Philology of the University of Barcelona (Spain). His research interests include the use of language corpora and (socio-) historical linguistics to investigate the mechanisms of language variation and change on a broad typological perspective.

**Kan Qian** is a Senior Lecturer in the School of Languages and Applied Linguistics, The Open University (UK). She has a PhD in Linguistics from Lancaster University, and is Senior Fellow of the British Higher Education Academy. Her research focusses on the use of technologies for the learning and teaching of languages: interactions in online discussion forums, mobile language learning and mobile application design, eTandem learning, and language MOOC design.

Notes on contributors

**Nathaniel Owen** is a Research Associate at the Open University. He has a PhD in language testing from the University of Leicester. He has published articles in peer-reviewed journals such as the International Journal of Research and Method in Education and book chapters in volumes such as The Routledge Handbook of English Language Teaching. He has experience of teaching English as a foreign language, with expertise in teaching EAP and exam preparation courses. He has previously worked as Senior Research Manager at Cambridge Assessment. He is currently participating in funded research projects with ETS and the British Council.

**Christine Pleines** is a Lecturer in German at the Open University's School of Languages and Applied Linguistics. She has a background in language learning and teaching and extensive experience in curriculum design and materials development. Her main interests are theories of second language development and all aspects of language pedagogy. Christine's research is in language learning in online environments and in learning through vicarious participation.

**Ursula Stickler** is a Senior Lecturer in German in the School of Languages and Applied Linguistics at the Open University, UK. Her research focusses on independent and technology enhanced language learning and teacher training. She has also published widely in the areas of tandem learning, qualitative methods for Computer Assisted Language Learning (CALL) research, and eyetracking. She is co-editor of the *System* Journal.

# Acknowledgements

We would like to express our gratitude to a number of people. First of all, to all the presenters and delegates who attended InnoConf 17 and made it such an interesting day. Secondly, to Carmen Álvarez-Mayo and Elia Lorena López, the previous conference organisers, who passed on their knowledge to make preparations easier. Thirdly, to all the authors who have contributed their work to this volume. We were honoured to count on the support of the many colleagues who acted as reviewers and provided open feedback on chapter drafts.

We would also like to express our gratitude to The Open University, specifically the School of Languages and Applied Linguistics for hosting the event and their logistical and financial support.

We would also like to thank Language Acts and Worldmaking for their contribution to the funding for this publication. Language Acts and Worldmaking is a flagship project funded by the AHRC Open World Research Initiative which aims to regenerate and transform modern language learning by foregrounding language's power to shape how we live and make our worlds. You can find out more about the project at https://languageacts.org/.

Finally, we would like to thank Sylvie Thouësny and Karine Fenix at Research-publishing.net for their help, support, enthusiasm, and patience.

      Fernando Rosell-Aguilar, Tita Beaven, and Mara Fuertes Gutiérrez

# 1 Integrating informal learning into formal language education: an introduction

**Fernando Rosell-Aguilar[1], Tita Beaven[2], and Mara Fuertes Gutiérrez[3]**

## 1. Introduction

This volume collects selected papers from the 2017 Innovative Language Teaching and Learning at University conference (InnoConf), which took place on the 16th of June at The Open University. The theme of the conference was *Integrating informal learning into formal language education*. The aim of the conference was to engage in productive collaboration between language professionals to further equip students to succeed in our ever-growing landscape of formal and informal learning. Given the unprecedented amount of online resources and communities available to language learners, the conference focussed on exploring how language teachers are integrating these opportunities into their settings.

This is the third volume in a series of books compiling papers from the InnoConf conferences. It follows from the first two volumes in 2015 and 2016 respectively: *Enhancing participation and collaboration* (Goria, Speicher, & Stollhans, 2016) and *Enhancing employability* (Álvarez-Mayo, Gallagher-Brett, & Michel, 2017).

---

1. The Open University, Milton Keynes, United Kingdom; fernando.rosell-aguilar@open.ac.uk

2. The Open University, Milton Keynes, United Kingdom; tita.beaven@open.ac.uk

3. The Open University, Milton Keynes, United Kingdom; mara.fuertes-gutierrez@open.ac.uk

How to cite this chapter: Rosell-Aguilar, F., Beaven, T., & Fuertes Gutiérrez, M. (2018). Integrating informal learning into formal language education: an introduction. In F. Rosell-Aguilar, T. Beaven, & M. Fuertes Gutiérrez (Eds), *Innovative language teaching and learning at university: integrating informal learning into formal language education* (pp. 1-6). Research-publishing.net. https://doi.org/10.14705/rpnet.2018.22.770

## 2.     InnoConf 17

The InnoConf 17 conference was hosted by the School of Languages and Applied Linguistics, and we were welcomed by Dr Regine Hampel, Professor of Open and Distance Language Learning and Associate Dean (Research & Scholarship) at the Faculty of Wellbeing, Education, and Language Studies at the Open University. Our first Keynote came from Dr Shannon Sauro, Associate Professor in the Department of Culture, Languages, and Media at Malmö University, Sweden. Her presentation, entitled *The Innovative and Creative Informal Language Learning of Fans*, explored the integration of fan practices into the university classroom to support language and literary learning.

The parallel presentations throughout the day introduced/displayed thought-provoking contributions from language teachers, researchers, and practitioners from different contexts in terms of languages taught, methodological approaches and pedagogical aims. The topics covered a large range of informal and formal learning initiatives for language learning, including the use of Whatsapp, language-learning mobile apps, Massive Open Online Courses (MOOCs), flipped learning, user-generated videos, intercultural exchanges and online immersion, collaborative writing, feedback, tandem learning, e-portfolios, and preparation for the year abroad.

The closing plenary followed a new format: conference organiser Tita Beaven conversed with Richard Simcott, a language consultant and life-long language learner who is a key player in the international polyglot movement, and one of the organisers of the Polyglot Conference. This format was well received by the conference participants and provided an engaging close to the day. Their conversation is captured in the final chapter of this book.

As well as the formal activities, it was a pleasure to have the opportunity to make new acquaintances, see 'old' faces, and engage in discussions on the many topics presented throughout the day. Social media (from the @Innoconf Twitter account and others) helped keep those who could not make it in person informed of the highlights of the day, as the #Innoconf17 led to interesting contributions and engagement.

## 3. Theme

The theme of the conference was *Integrating informal learning into formal language education*. Web technologies have enabled learners to access teaching materials outside the boundaries of the classroom. Whether through desktop computers or mobile devices, the wealth of resources available has multiplied in the last few years, allowing learners to access learning objects at their convenience. At the same time, "learning has become increasingly self-directed and often occurs away from schools and other formal educational settings" (Song & Lee, 2014, p. 511). As contact time with students is increasingly reduced in higher education, teachers are looking at ways to support their students with resources that can be used outside the classroom. This means that many teachers are looking at approaches such as *flipping* the classroom, designed to free up time in class to concentrate on activities that foster interaction by enabling students to engage independently with tasks which do not require supervision, such as completing grammar drilling exercises or using authentic materials (text, audio, video) – in the case of languages. Other initiatives include the use of social media to access resources or interact with peers or native speakers, telecollaboration activities between learners in different countries, or the co-creation of learning artefacts such as videos, websites, or texts.

The incorporation of such activities into the curriculum blurs the boundaries between formal and informal activity, and as conference organisers, we wanted to bring this theme to the fore at InnoConf 17.

## 4. Organisation of the book and chapter overview

### 4.1. Learning collaboratively online: attitudes, motivation, and learning communities

The first section of the book is entitled *Learning collaboratively online: attitudes, motivation, and learning communities*. Under this heading, we find four chapters that expand our knowledge of how learners feel about the use of different types of software for language learning purposes across formal, semi-formal, and informal contexts. **Bárkányi** ponders the assumed informal nature of learning through Language MOOCs (LMOOCs) and whether learners perceive participating in activities in such environments as an informal activity with a lesser degree of performance anxiety or not. Through a large-scale study of LMOOC learners, she finds very positive attitudes, but also a certain degree of anxiety. Within a more formal context, **Martínez-Carrasco** presents his findings from a study into the use of Wikis for L2 collaborative writing by 103 learners from Spain. As well as positive results in terms of language acquisition and impressions from the learners, his study also reports improvements in terms of collaboration and socialisation among students. The third chapter moves to another type of software: **Saona-Vallejos** examines how a range of students across different language levels rate the *busuu* language learning mobile application, focussing on its features, design, and social aspects. In addition, he carried out tests on written and oral skill improvements and concludes that the vast majority of participants had improved in their written performance, but not their oral skills. Closing this section, **Wang** describes the results of his research into tandem learning exchanges. The participants in his study perceive their participation in the exchanges as a useful complement to classroom learning, as well as appreciating the opportunities for interpersonal communication and developing cultural awareness through these – however, participation was low and Wang considers the implications of his approach for future research.

## 4.2. Testing and evaluating language learning tools

This second section of the book, *Testing and evaluating language learning tools*, focusses on the evaluation of innovative technologies and resources in a range of settings. **Cervi-Wilson** and **Brick** used *ImparApp*, a location-based game designed for mobile devices, to extend their students' language learning beyond the classroom. They present the design of the app activities, which take the students around the city they study in to discover its roman past, and the results of their first evaluation. **Mericka** also reports on a study which saw her students going out of the classroom to extend their learning. The students worked collaboratively to create LipDub videos based on German songs. Although the videos were different from what the author expected, they were later used as resources for further learning in class and her participants rated the activities positively. **Chen** developed a series of videos to support her students' Chinese studies using a flipped classroom approach. The videos covered grammar rules, vocabulary use, and explanation of texts, and students could watch them before or after class. The students who used the videos showed a preference for grammar videos and Chen discusses the implications of her study for further design of resources and management of flipped classroom activities. **Salin** introduces the *Better French Living Project,* an initiative to prepare students for their year abroad by developing their practical and intercultural knowledge as well as enhancing their listening skills outside the classroom. The resources selected for the project helped students deal with some practical challenges, such as securing accommodation or opening a bank account, as well as introducing topics such as cultural differences and stereotyping. Her students rated the resources and activities related to them positively and the author suggests further research is needed to evaluate their impact after the students return from their stays abroad. **Vacas Matos** offers her perspective from a formal setting. Her students engaged with native speakers to create a series of videos to feed into a multimodal corpus of informal speech acts in Spanish to teach pragmatics. The results show that, although participants had different levels in terms of language level, there were no differences in their pragmatic behaviour. The author concludes with a series of suggestions for further use of the corpus to teach pragmatics in the foreign language classroom. Finally, **Rosell-Aguilar** presents an overview of the identified potential of Twitter as a language learning tool and the evidence found so far to support its use. Although research so far has focussed on initiatives carried out in formal settings, the author argues for further research in informal contexts.

## 4.3. The polyglot community: an interview with Richard Simcott

This final section records the second keynote from InnoConf 17. **Beaven** and **Simcott** had an engaging conversation about plurilingualism, language teaching and learning in the context of the changing technological landscape, and the development of new communities and networks to support learning 'in the wild'.

## 5. Conclusion

The chapters in this book provide insights into many types of innovative approaches to teaching languages at university and beyond. The contributing authors have experimented with new strategies to enrich their students' learning experience or identified new ways of using existing resources in and outside the classroom. The experiences reported and evaluated in the book are by no means exhaustive, and much work continues to be undertaken by language professionals everywhere. InnoConf 18 and further InnoConf conferences will continue to explore these themes and offer opportunities for language professionals to share ideas, resources, successes, and failures with the goal of improving our practice. That is a mission worth sharing.

## References

Álvarez-Mayo, C., Gallagher-Brett, A., & Michel, F. (Eds). (2017). *Innovative language teaching and learning at university: enhancing employability*. Research-publishing.net. https://doi.org/10.14705/rpnet.2017.innoconf2016.9781908416506

Goria, C., Speicher, O., & Stollhans, S. (Eds). (2016). *Innovative language teaching and learning at university: enhancing participation and collaboration*. Research-publishing.net. https://doi.org/10.14705/rpnet.2016.9781908416322

Song, D., & Lee, J. (2014). Has Web 2.0 revitalized informal learning? The relationship between Web 2.0 and informal learning. *Journal of Computer Assisted Learning, 30*(6), 511-533. https://doi.org/10.1111/jcal.12056

# Section 1.

# Learning collaboratively online: attitudes, motivation, and learning communities

# 2 Can you teach me to speak? Oral practice and anxiety in a language MOOC

## Zsuzsanna Bárkányi[1]

### Abstract

The present chapter examines learners' beliefs and attitudes with regard to speaking in a learning environment that is neither formal nor non-formal. The main research question is whether learners perceive Language Massive Open Online Courses (LMOOCs) as a completely informal context that is free of anxiety or rather as a virtual classroom where Foreign Language classroom Anxiety (FLA) (Horwitz, Horwitz, & Cope, 1986) is present. Data were obtained from over 200 beginner learners on self-reflective questionnaires and forum discussions. Results indicate that learners have a positive attitude towards language learning on LMOOCs, but FLA is present in this asynchronous speaking environment too and needs to be addressed by the course instructors.

Keywords: LMOOCs, Spanish, foreign language anxiety, informal learning.

## 1. Introduction

Massive Open Online Courses (MOOCs) can be perceived to be half-way between formal and non-formal learning. On the one hand, they are formal in that they have a structured, pre-designed content, and are facilitated by an instructor and offered by an educational institution. On the other hand, they are self-paced, occur outside the classroom, are usually not accredited, and imply a

---

1. The Open University, Milton Keynes, United Kingdom; zsuzsanna.barkanyi@open.ac.uk

How to cite this chapter: Bárkányi, Z. (2018). Can you teach me to speak? Oral practice and anxiety in a language MOOC. In F. Rosell-Aguilar, T. Beaven, & M. Fuertes Gutiérrez (Eds), *Innovative language teaching and learning at university: integrating informal learning into formal language education* (pp. 9-16). Research-publishing.net. https://doi.org/10.14705/rpnet.2018.22.771

leisurely activity for many learners, all of which are features that characterise informal learning.

LMOOCs are unique among MOOCs in that language learning is mainly skill-based rather than only knowledge-based (Bárcena & Martín-Monje, 2015; Halliday, 1993), and acquiring these skills necessarily involves interaction with other speakers. The importance of affective factors, such as motivation and anxiety, in these interactions and in L2 acquisition in general, has long been recognised. The term Foreign Language Anxiety was created by Horwitz et al. (1986) and refers to a specific type of anxiety that learners might experience across all language activities. The least anxiety-provoking language learning activity is reading comprehension (MacIntyre, Noels, & Clément, 1997) while the most anxiety-provoking one is speaking (e.g. Koch & Terrell, 1991; Young, 1990, 1999). Most researchers agree that FLA has a negative impact on learners' performance (see MacIntyre, 2017, and the references therein).

Research shows that online environments and Computer-Mediated-Communication (CMC) might create low anxiety language learning contexts which are beneficial for many learners (Cooke-Plagwitz, 2008; Rosell-Aguilar, 2005, among others). There are few studies addressing the development of speaking skills in online learning environments. Rodrigues and Vethamani (2015) showed that learners in an online conversation programme with synchronous sessions showed bigger improvement in their speaking skills than the control group. Jauregi et al. (2011) found significant effects for CMC in willingness to speak with native speakers. Rubio (2015) examined the gains in pronunciation and comprehensibility on an LMOOC vs. on a face-to-face (f2f) course and concluded that improvement was larger on the LMOOC, mostly owing to the amount and types of feedback. Melchor-Couto (2016) and Reinders and Wattana (2015) demonstrated that language learners performing oral interaction activities in virtual world contexts exhibited lower anxiety levels than in traditional classroom settings. Thus, LMOOCs with no f2f interaction and no synchronous CMC present an interesting environment to observe affective variables such as FLA which is often experienced in classroom settings.

## 2. Method

The Spanish for Beginners Programme offered by The Open University on FutureLearn comprises six four-week courses with four to six hours of study per week covering the syllabus at A1 of the CEFR. Qualitative data was collected from over 200 learners on the first presentation of the Spanish for Beginners 3 course through open-ended questions on reflective questionnaires and discussions in the forums. The texts obtained in this way were thematically coded and analysed. At this point, a descriptive and exploratory approach was taken and a manual process followed. The emerging topics were highlighted and organised into broader thematic categories. Discourse referring to FLA was divided into sub-themes to gain a better understanding and a comprehensive view of learners' anxiety levels. In the present chapter, we analyse the responses and comments referring to the attitudes regarding the speaking activities proposed in the LMOOC. Note that spoken interactions in this learning environment are asynchronous, they consist of recording one's voice and uploading the file in the discussion forum, for instance, describing your daily activities or answering to audio prompts.

## 3. Results and discussion

### 3.1. Learner attitudes

Most learners had positive feelings towards language learning and the acquisition of speaking skills on our LMOOC under scrutiny; 79.43% of our respondents indicated that listening and speaking skills can be learnt in this context just as well as reading and writing skills. Half of the participants (45.96%) completed the speaking tasks, i.e. the recording activities, however, when it came to sharing them on the discussion forum only 21.49% did so. The reasons for not uploading their recordings fall into three broad categories: (1) technical issues, (2) lack of motivation, and (3) anxiety. Technical issues generally involve the lack of adequate equipment (e.g. a microphone) and lack of familiarity with recording tools. Learners were often hesitant to share their recordings because they thought that they would not receive feedback or would not receive appropriate

Chapter 2

constructive feedback. The use of adjectives like *intimidating, not confident enough, embarrassed, shy*, etc. indicate varying levels of speaking anxiety.

### 3.2. Foreign language anxiety

Learners' comments reflect that they were not confident enough to record themselves or they felt intimidated and embarrassed to upload their recordings. In many cases, a high level of anxiety can be observed in the comments of those students too who did complete the speaking tasks. Comments belonging to this group have been coded and analysed according to topic, which resulted in three major categories: (1) humour, (2) expressions of effort, and (3) explicit expressions of 'classroom' anxiety.

Humour is well-known for being helpful in adverse situations. It has been observed (e.g. Demjén, 2016) that people with serious illnesses in life-threatening situations often use humorous discourse to talk about frightening, sensitive, taboo experiences to alleviate the psychological impact of their condition. FLA is far from a life-threatening condition, however, a number of comments in the discussion forum contain humorous discourse, especially self-irony to reduce anxiety. Comments like "I think it will require more listening as I can roll my rr's but I sound like a drunken lowlander singing" show that humour is helpful in distancing from the embarrassment as if it was not the learner who has a problem with the pronunciation of the *r* sound in Spanish, but a drunken lowlander. At the same time, the opportunity to laugh together gives a feeling of collective empowerment in a situation where the speaker feels less powerful. The feeling of a supportive learning community is an essential component of a successful and enjoyable learning experience and is encouraged and facilitated by the instructors of the beginners' Spanish courses.

Reflections on the learning effort like "Struggled with the pronunciation, but I tried, and that's what counts" also provoke supportive comments from peers like "I really like your pronunciation", "well done", "we must practise" which no doubt helps reduce the anxiety involved in exposing oneself as well as the potential feelings of being laughed at. It also helps building a sense of a cohesive learning community.

Research indicates that language learners feel they perform better when interactions are via computer rather than f2f (Henderson, Huang, Grant, & Henderson, 2009). Similar conclusions have been found for FLA research. Ahangari and Sioofy (2013) found that a group of students who participated on a course where cooperative learning was integrated into computer-assisted language learning had a significant improvement in FLA when compared to other groups where no computer-assisted language learning occurred. Bárkányi and Melchor-Couto (2017) also observe that learners on an LMOOC find computer-mediated interactions less stressful than f2f communication. Despite the advantages of the computer-shielded learning environment, comments reveal anxiety with regard to speaking: e.g. "I'm still nervous about fellow students (strangers seems wrong to say) hearing my voice", "sorry for my pronunciation", and "please excuse my pronunciation". Note that learners on our LMOOC hardly ever apologise for other language-skills like grammar or vocabulary.

## 3.3. Limitations of the study

Although our study has reached its aim in exploring FLA on LMOOCs, there were some unavoidable limitations regarding data collection. As participation in forum discussions and in the reflective pre- and post-course questionnaires was voluntary, our conclusions do not necessarily reflect the whole learning community of the course under scrutiny. Furthermore, post-course surveys typically have a 10% response rate as compared to pre-course surveys, and respondents often skip questions which results in uneven data.

## 3.4. What can instructors do?

Similarly to traditional classroom settings, the treatment of FLA in online contexts such as the language MOOC that is the subject of this study might involve:

- Skill-building activities, as higher levels of competence usually enhance confidence (MacIntyre & Gardner, 1991); Bárkányi and Melchor-Couto (2017) show in a small-scale study that skill-building increases self-ratings on LMOOCs too.

- Awareness raising: pointing out that incorrect output also implies knowledge and helps learners form realistic goals.

- Regulating emotions: identifying false beliefs regarding speaking and encouraging appropriate risk-taking (Bekleyen, 2004).

- Constructive and encouraging feedback on pronunciation and spoken productions is also very much appreciated by learners as this comment shows: "thank you for all the encouragement. The course is great and I'm loving every minute of it – so xenoglossophobia has gone :-)".

## 4. Conclusions

This chapter shows that LMOOC learners have positive attitudes towards acquiring speaking skills in this type of learning environment. Although speaking activities are not synchronous and thus do not involve f2f communication, most learners report feeling intimidated or embarrassed by the option of having to post their recordings. Learners who have the courage to complete the speaking activities often use various discourse strategies to alleviate the psychological burden of speaking anxiety. This clearly demonstrates that FLA is not only present in f2f classrooms but also on non-formal asynchronous online courses, where it can similarly have an inhibitory effect too, but generally to a lesser degree than in the f2f classroom.

## References

Ahangari, S., & Sioofy, M. (2013). The effect of computer assisted cooperative language learning on Iranian high school students' language anxiety and reading comprehension. *International Journal of Foreign Language Teaching & Research, 1*(3), 34-47.

Bárcena, E., & and Martín-Monje, E. (2015). Introduction: language MOOCs: an emerging field. In E. Martín-Monje & E. Bárcena (Eds), *Language MOOCs: providing learning, transcending boundaries* (pp. 1-15). De Gruyter.

Bárkányi, Z., & and Melchor-Couto, S. (2017). Foreign language anxiety on a massive open online language course. In K. Borthwick, L. Bradley & S. Thouësny (Eds), *CALL in a climate of change: adapting to turbulent global conditions – short papers from EUROCALL 2017* (pp. 24-29). Research-publishing.net. https://doi.org/10.14705/rpnet.2017.eurocall2017.683

Bekleyen, N. (2004). Foreign language anxiety. *Çukurova Üniversitesi Sosyal Bilimler Enstitüsü Dergisi, 13*(2), 27-44.

Cooke-Plagwitz, J. (2008). New directions in CALL: an objective introduction to Second Life. *CALICO Journal, 25*(3), 547-557. https://doi.org/10.1558/cj.v25i3.547-557

Demjén, Z. (2016). Laughing at cancer: humour, empowerment, solidarity and coping online. *Journal of Pragmatics, 101*, 18-30. https://doi.org/10.1016/j.pragma.2016.05.010

Halliday, M. A. K. (1993). Towards a language-based theory of learning. *Linguistics and Education, 5*(2), 93-116. https://doi.org/10.1016/0898-5898(93)90026-7

Henderson, M., Huang, H., Grant, S., & Henderson, L. (2009). Language Acquisition in *Second Life*: Improving Self-efficacy Beliefs. In R. J. Atkinson & C. McBeath (Eds), *Same places, different spaces. Proceedings Ascilite Auckland 2009*. University of Auckland.

Horwitz, E. K., Horwitz, M. B., & Cope, J. (1986). Foreign language classroom anxiety. *The Modern Language Journal, 70*(2), 125-132. https://doi.org/10.1111/j.1540-4781.1986.tb05256.x

Jauregi, K., Canto, S., de Graaf, R., Koenraad, T., & Moonen, M. (2011). Verbal interaction in Second Life: towards a pedagogic framework to task design. *Computer Assisted Language Learning, 24*(1), 77-101. https://doi.org/10.1080/09588221.2010.538699

Koch, A. S., & Terrell, T. D. (1991). Affective reactions of foreign language students to natural approach activities and teaching techniques. In: Horwitz, D. K. and Young, D. J. (Eds), *Language anxiety: From theory and practice to classroom implications*. Upper Saddle River: Prentice-Hall, pp. 109–126.

MacIntyre, P. D. (2017). *New insights into language anxiety: theory, research and educational implications (second language acquisition)*. Multilingual Matters.

MacIntyre, P. D., & Gardner, R. C. (1991). Methods and results in the study of anxiety and language learning: a review of the literature. *Language Learning, 41*(1), 85-117. https://doi.org/10.1111/j.1467-1770.1991.tb00677.x

MacIntyre, P. D., Noels, K. A., & Clément, R. (1997). Biases in self ratings of second language proficiency: the role of language anxiety. *Language Learning, 47*(2), 265-287. https://doi.org/10.1111/0023-8333.81997008

Melchor-Couto, S. (2016). Foreign language anxiety levels in Second Life oral interaction. *ReCALL, 29*(1), 99-119. https://doi.org/10.1017/S0958344016000185

Reinders, H., & Wattana, S. (2015). Affect and willingness to communicate in digital game-based learning. *ReCALL, 27*(1), 38-57. https://doi.org/10.1017/S0958344014000226

Rodrigues, P. D., & Vethamani, M. E. (2015). The impact of online learning in the development of speaking skills. *Journal of Interdisciplinary Research in Education, 5*(1), 43-67.

Rosell-Aguilar, F. (2005). Task design for audiographic conferencing: promoting beginner oral interaction in distance language learning. *Computer-Assisted Language Learning, 18*(5), 417-442. https://doi.org/10.1080/09588220500442772

Rubio, F. (2015). Teaching pronunciation and comprehensibility in a Language MOOC. In E. Bárcena & E. Marín-Monje (Eds), *Language MOOCs: providing learning, transcending boundaries* (pp. 143-160). De Gruyter.

Young, D. J. (1990). An investigation of students' perspectives on anxiety and speaking. *Foreign Language Annals, 23*(6), 539-553. https://doi.org/10.1111/j.1944-9720.1990.tb00424.x

Young, D. J. (1999). *Affect in foreign language and second language learning: a practical guide to creating a low-anxiety classroom atmosphere.* McGraw-Hill.

# 3. Social media in L2 education: exploring on-line collaborative writing in EFL settings

## Robert Martínez-Carrasco[1]

## Abstract

This paper presents a classroom experience regarding the use of wikis in L2 collaborative writing settings. Framed in the current post-positivist educational climate in higher education, the adoption of wikis as a Technology-Enhanced Language Learning (TELL) platform complements and enriches the classroom-based interaction of L2 learners. While developing solid L2 writing and self-expression skills, wikis may be said to foster other related core abilities – reading and comprehension, critical thinking, exegetic skills, integration of culture-specific elements in foreign language learning, and use of new technologies, etc. In the process of drafting culture-bound texts, the co-creating students become aware of the weight of cultural elements in their texts in an asynchronous, cross-cultural communication process, and they are able to bridge the cultural divide not only through non-formal, peer-to-peer learning, but also through empowered cross-cultural understanding in a truly emancipating English as a Foreign Language (EFL) setting.

Keywords: collaborative writing, wikis, TELL, digital pedagogy, informal learning.

## 1. Introduction

The way literacy is understood in contemporary settings, following the rapid implementation of ever-changing information and communication

1. Jaume I University, Castelló de la Plana, Spain; rcarrasc@uji.es

**How to cite this chapter:** Martínez-Carrasco, R. (2018). Social media in L2 education: exploring on-line collaborative writing in EFL settings. In F. Rosell-Aguilar, T. Beaven, & M. Fuertes Gutiérrez (Eds), *Innovative language teaching and learning at university: integrating informal learning into formal language education* (pp. 17-26). Research-publishing.net. https://doi.org/10.14705/rpnet.2018.22.772

technologies, requires particular awareness of the new types of discourses and social practices that justify the introduction of TELL platforms in the L2 classroom (Chun, Smith, & Kern, 2016). Indeed, in the socialisation of L2 students, innovative technology-enhanced writing tools – wikis, blogs, Google Docs, etc. – have expanded the range, scope, and possibilities of contemporary collaboration (Yim & Warschauer, 2017, p. 147), reinforcing the cognitive, post-positivist turn in higher education characterised by situated practices in student-centred environments where procedural knowledge (*knowing how*) and the integrated mobilisation of clusters of competences seem to be gaining increasing momentum. This approach has undoubtedly allowed students to resort to non-formal and informal activities and platforms to round their learning experience.

Indeed, the introduction of technologies in the classroom may be said to have blurred, in a way, some of the boundaries between formal, informal, and non-formal education. While the literature has explored the three concepts extensively and has suggested many a definition, the educational implications of contemporary digital pedagogy seem to complicate the narrative, suggesting that informal and formal learning are part of a continuum in every technology-enhanced learning situation (Lai, Khaddage, & Knezek, 2013). Instead, it is the intention and the structure of the learning experience that characterises the debate, since most technologically enhanced pedagogical approaches reflect varying degrees of formality and informality simultaneously, and therefore they both have an impact on the learning experience of students.

Wikis, as Elola and Oskoz (2010) argue, "provide learners with a tool to create, transform, and erase their work with built-in accountability" (p. 53), which affects the motivation of students and triggers a significant number of valuable skills, namely content mastery, self-confidence, autonomy, and group work, among others. At the same time, wikis may serve as a platform for cross-cultural awareness and communication, reflecting on the power relations that shape the meaning negotiation processes following the interaction of two socio-cultural communities.

## 2. Introducing Wikipedia in the L2 classroom

"As a ground-breaking and interdisciplinary phenomenon", Alonso (2015, p. 90) argues, Wikipedia has attracted the attention of researchers from many fields, including communication, politics, and language. Indeed, Wikipedia has become, for many, a platform to situate their teaching practices and unfold a plethora of activities that may suit the most varied fields, specifically in the L2 classroom: critical analysis of articles, article correction and revision, article creation, article expansion and improvement, and translation of articles, etc. (Lerga & Aibar, 2015).

Wikimedia Foundation is well aware of the possibilities Wikipedia offers to the post-positivist classroom, and indeed a number of its affiliates have implemented several educational projects, be it through the many specific sections within the online encyclopaedia where resources and educational content are brought together (Lerga & Aibar, 2015, p. 3) or through Wikiprojects, that is, teams of users working for a common objective. Besides, the Wikimedia Educational Portal, a wiki aimed at coordinating and spreading educational activities and projects across the world, was created for anyone interested in using Wikipedia for educational purposes (Lerga & Aibar, 2015, p. 4), linking global projects, spreading new initiatives and resources, etc. Launched back in 2010, the portal serves as a coordination meeting point for educators and students with the support, resources, and practical information Wikimedia offers.

## 3. The project

### 3.1. Motivation

The classroom experience below elaborates on those premises and introduces Wikipedia as a platform for collaborative writing and inter-cultural awareness. The participants involved, 13 males and 93 females, were all foreign speakers of English enrolled in the module 'English language for translators and interpreters' corresponding to the second year of the degree in Translation and Interpreting offered by Jaume I University (Spain). The overall objective of the course was for students to reach a C1 level of English according to the Common European Framework of languages (CEFR). Following a holistic methodology, the project sought the progressive, culturally-aware socialisation of students through the introduction of real discursive practices in the L2 classroom, mobilising a substantial number of the so-called 'generic competences' reflected in the Tuning Project (González & Wagenaar, 2003), a European initiative started in 2000 as a way to link the political objectives of the Bologna Process and the Lisbon Strategy to the higher educational sector and the Common European Framework: emancipation, creativity, motivation, responsibility, empowerment, and autonomy, etc. In this particular case, beside the module-specific competences related to linguistic and discursive proficiency in L2, the wiki-project presented along these pages addressed most of the generic competences (Table 1) included in Muñoz Raya (2004).

Table 1. Generic competences explored throughout wiki-project

| Personal generic competences | Instrumental generic competences |
|---|---|
| • Ethic commitment | • Knowledge of a foreign language |
| • Critical reasoning | • Planning and time management |
| • Appreciation of diversity and multiculturality | • Decision making |
| | • Problem solving |
| • Interpersonal skills | • Capacity for analysis and synthesis |
| • Teamwork | • Use of information and communications technology |
| • Leadership | |
| | • Information management skills |
| **Systemic generic competences** | **Other generic competences** |
| • Concern for quality | • Capacity for applying knowledge in practice |
| • Capacity to learn | |
| • Capacity to adapt to new situations | • Ability to work on their own |
| • Creativity | • Project design and management |

## 3.2. Setting up the project

Students were asked to create, in groups of five members, an expository text aimed at a global audience that reflected part of their cultural background and identity: something related to the festivities and festivals of their hometowns, traditions, or gastronomy, etc. The underlying rationale was twofold: on the one hand, to focus on text production, discursive practices, and language proficiency collaboratively; developing a number of strategies and competences that complement individual work. On the other, to make students aware of the situated nature of both linguistic and cultural practices, since it is when students are faced with the difficulties of conveying culture-specific references in their texts that they reflect on the cultural load inherent to language and culture. Wrongly understood as factual systems, students confront the idea that languages, as semiological systems, condition speakers in the way they apprehend reality around them, and therefore condition their linguistic and cultural practices. Consequently, in order to address text production successfully, students realised that they needed to implement a number of strategies in order to bridge the cultural gap (paraphrases, use of loans, calques, and neologisms, etc.).

Students were told that their text was to be drafted and modified on the wiki space, and therefore all communication among group members or between groups would take place via the wiki. Similarly, students were reminded that the project would take place exclusively outside the classroom as an ongoing group project. No guidelines were given regarding the way to work. Students were allowed to decide how they would address their collaborative writing process: synchronously or asynchronously, dividing the text into sub-sections drafted individually or working together on each and every sub-section, etc. The rationale behind that decision was for the researcher to explore the patterns of collaboration that emerge naturally when students are faced with such collaborative tasks. Focus group interviews in which students were asked to explain why they had opted for a given particular approach were recorded at the end of the project.

Chapter 3

The different changes in the articles were monitored in the history page of the wiki, which made it possible for the lecturer to analyse the evolution of texts and the way students created, edited, and negotiated the relevant content and structure of their text. When it came to group formation, students were told that all members in a group should have a similar level of English, even if it was up to the group to make the decision. Similarly, since students approached text production as a team, they were assessed as a team. Once the first draft of the texts was ready, the texts were distributed among the groups for peer revision and correction. Students were encouraged to revise the texts, looking for areas for improvement in the overall text production process. Before submitting the final draft, students were asked to evaluate the suggestions by their peers, accepting or rejecting them accordingly. In case they did not agree with the corrections, the groups were encouraged to discuss the different options available until a common solution was found, fostering further asynchronous collaboration and interaction. The lecturer assessed the final drafts, thus completing the project.

## 4. Methodology and data collection

The project relies on critical pragmatist grounds, conceiving education as something in constant re-negotiation and interpretation, influenced by power relations within society.

In order to measure and study both the quality of the resulting texts and the impressions of the students, a number of strategies were implemented. On the one hand, focus group interviews where the students reflected on the overall process and their perceptions regarding both collaborative writing and the use of wikis. On the other hand, an analysis of their texts was carried out at two levels. First of all, in order to measure the quality of the texts for classroom purposes, the Writing Assessment Scale by Cambridge English Language Assessment was applied. The rubric, divided in four sub-scales (content, communicative achievement, organisation, and language) helped students understand their actual command of English and the different aspects they should be working on for future written assignments. For research purposes, a deeper textual analysis is currently taking place regarding the type of mistakes students make not only when they write collaboratively but also when they are asked to revise the texts drafted by their peers: the level of awareness they display regarding what constitutes a valid/not valid piece of writing and the particular elements they systematically detect or deem more important, etc.

Regarding the focus group interviews, students were asked a number of questions related to collaboration in L2 settings, the use of wikis, and other technology-enhanced elements in the L2 classroom, and their own perceptions of whether such activities are of any use in foreign language education. The results appear to back prior literature regarding the use of wikis in the L2 classroom. Indeed, all focus groups mention systematically four areas of remarkable satisfaction: motivation, deeper and more effective socialisation, greater command of their L2, and the positive impact of peer scaffolding. The following two extracts by two female students in two different groups summarise the general opinion of the participating students regarding the usefulness and their perceptions of the collaborative learning experience:

> "To be honest, I hate working in groups. It makes things much more difficult because you need to make sure that all your timetables match. The good thing of wikis is that we didn't have to work online at the same time, so we could see the change history and leave messages for our classmates as we were writing. At the beginning I thought that using a wiki would complicate things unnecessarily, but after a while we all got into it. I mean, this is not the typical essay you are asked to write in an English class. It is a longer project, and we even had to include audio-visual materials, videos and links to other websites and stuff, and that was interesting. I think it was much more interesting than a typical essay just because of that: it was real, it was more 'out there', more interactive" (Student 1).

> "We should be doing this kind of assignments [sic] more often. Because this was English, but at the same time it was computing, and research,

Chapter 3

and sometimes there were disagreements and we had to find a solution. And because we knew that you would be reading the change history we did everything in English, which was difficult but at the same time it was a challenge. When we were revising the contributions by the other students sometimes we couldn't explain why something was a mistake so I had to check grammar books and everything in order to make my point. And then, how do you tell them that what they wrote is not correct? I had to think of ways of letting them know without being, like, bossy" (Student 2).

## 5. Discussion and conclusions

The classroom experience presented above, in line with similar studies (Aydın & Yıldız, 2014; Sabet, Tahriri, & Pasand, 2013), elaborates on the impact of asynchronous wiki-based work in the L2 classroom as a means to complement the coursework of the module. As the preliminary results of the focus group interviews attest, the positive impact students perceive in their command of their L2 through collaborative wiki-based writing is generally believed to result in higher levels of motivation when learning a foreign language, which confirms previous similar experiences by Roschelle et al. (2001), among others. At the same time, the wiki-project is believed to strengthen, in full agreement with Yang (2014), the progressive socialisation process of students in their respective discursive communities, another aspect noted consistently among the participating students.

This way, the use of wikis empowers students to create, transform, and shape their texts collaboratively in a flexible learning environment that allows the lecturer to scaffold the learning curve of their students while they work outside the classroom, supervising the project and making sure that a number of general and module-specific competences are developed. Besides, the use of wikis seems to foster further collaboration and peer scaffolding in joint processes of meaning negotiation and text production, which enhances the overall learning process of L2 learners. This, however, should be corroborated by more in-depth studies on the patterns and nature of collaboration (power relations within group members, etc.) and how those patterns change as the students progress and attain higher levels in their L2. The analysis of the focus group interviews seems to indicate that students tend to 'avoid' collaboration and divide texts in sections to be drafted individually, posing problems in terms of overall quality of the text, coherence, etc.

As Greenhow and Lewin (2016) suggest, there is a lack of current models that theorise social media as a space for informal learning, even if technology and social media have the potential to complement and enrich the educational picture "through greater agency, opportunities to participate in networked communities and access to a wide range of resources to support knowledge building and collaboration" (p. 6). Incorporating elements of digital pedagogy in the L2 classroom, as reflected above, may serve as a starting point for students to collaborate outside the language module, build bridges between formal, informal, and non-formal learning, and realise that foreign language education needs to be approached in a comprehensive manner. This requires both traditional, classroom-based interaction and other non-formal and informal elements that help tackle the situated, complex nature of languages, the very first and last barrier that students encounter when trying to access any foreign language.

## Acknowledgements

This classroom experience was supported by a teaching innovation grant to 3470/17 Translating Wikipedia back and forth. A professional endeavour at Jaume I University.

## References

Alonso, E. (2015). Analysing the use and perception of Wikipedia in the professional context of translation. *The Journal of Specialised Translation, 23*, 89-116.

Aydın, Z., & Yıldız, S. (2014). Use of wikis to promote collaborative EFL writing. *Language Learning & Technology, 18*(181), 160-180.

Chun, D., Smith, B., & Kern, R. (2016). Technology in language use, language teaching, and language learning. *Modern Language Journal, 100*, 64-80. https://doi.org/10.1111/modl.12302

Elola, I., & Oskoz, A. (2010). Collaborative writing : fostering foreign language and writing conventions development. *Language Learning & Technology*, 14(3), 51-71.

González, J., & Wagenaar, R. (2003). *Tuning. Final report*. Bilbao.

Greenhow, C., & Lewin, C. (2016). Social media and education: reconceptualizing the boundaries of formal and informal learning. *Learning, Media and Technology, 4*(1), 6-30. https://doi.org/10.1080/17439884.2015.1064954

Lai, K.W., Khaddage, F., & Knezek, G. (2013). Blending student technology experiences in formal and informal learning. *Journal of Computer Assisted Learning, 29*(5), 414-425. https://doi.org/10.1111/jcal.12030

Lerga, M., & Aibar, E. (2015). Best practice guide to use Wikipedia in university education.

Muñoz Raya, E. (Ed.). (2004). *Libro blanco. Título de Grado de Traducción e Interpretación*. Agencia Nacional de Evaluación de la Calidad y Acreditación. https://goo.gl/5FvT3W

Roschelle, J., Pea, R. D., Hoadley, C. M., Gordin, D. N., & Means, B. (2001). Changing how and what children want to learn in school with computer-based technologies. *The Future of Children, 10*(2), 76-101. https://doi.org/10.2307/1602690

Sabet, M. K., Tahriri, A., & Pasand, P. G. (2013). The impact of peer scaffolding through process approach on EFL learners' academic writing fluency. *Theory and Practice in Language Studies, 3*(10), 1893-1901. https://doi.org/10.4304/tpls.3.10.1893-1901

Yang, L. (2014). Examining the mediational means in collaborative writing: case studies of undergraduate ESL students in business courses. *Journal of Second Language Writing, 23*, 74-89. https://doi.org/10.1016/j.jslw.2014.01.003

Yim, S., & Warschauer, M. (2017). Web-based collaborative writing in L2 contexts: methodological insights from text mining. *Language Learning & Technology, 21*(1), 146-165.

# 4. Busuu: how do users rate this app for language learning?

## Miguel Ángel Saona-Vallejos[1]

### Abstract

Busuu (https://www.busuu.com) is one of several existing Social Networking Sites for Language Learning (SNSLLs). According to Álvarez (2016), it has all the features an SNSLL should have. However, once Busuu migrated to a mobile compatible platform in 2016, it lost some of the social aspects of a Social Networking Site (SNS) determined by Boyd and Ellison (2008) and Duffy (2011). As the most used language learning platform worldwide (Busuu, n.d), the user experience of its learners is of interest to the field of Computer-Assisted Language Learning (CALL). A pilot study to see how users rate it was conducted at an English university for four weeks. This chapter shows the results of that research.

Keywords: ICTs, Busuu, social networking sites, SNSLLs, informal language learning.

## 1. Introduction

Busuu defines itself as "the world's largest social network for language learning, providing courses in 12 different languages on web and mobile to more than 70 million learners worldwide" (Busuu, n.d). Busuu learners can train their language skills through self-paced learning units following the Common European Framework of Reference for languages (CEFR), from A1 to B2 levels.

---

1. University of Central Lancashire, Preston, United Kingdom; masaona-vallejos@uclan.ac.uk

**How to cite this chapter:** Saona-Vallejos, M. Á. (2018). Busuu: how do users rate this app for language learning? In F. Rosell-Aguilar, T. Beaven, & M. Fuertes Gutiérrez (Eds), *Innovative language teaching and learning at university: integrating informal learning into formal language education* (pp. 27-36). Research-publishing.net. https://doi.org/10.14705/rpnet.2018.22.773

The platform offers three different versions on the web and for mobile devices: free, premium, and professional.

The issue of social interaction on SNSs has been the topic of some research. Blattner and Lomicka (2012) suggested that the social interaction that takes place in such environments helps students to develop their pragmatic competence. Previously, Lee (2006) argued that the frequency of use of those SNSs has a positive impact on learners' oral proficiency, vocabulary acquisition, and syntactic complexity.

In contrast, it is important to underline that even if students may not receive enough grammar instruction from these SNSLLs, according to Lin, Warschauer, and Blake (2016), they still feel they make significant improvements, because, for most of them, this is the first experience of using their L2 in meaningful conversations with others. Nonetheless, as Jones (2001) had pointed out before, it may be difficult to engage users over a long period without teachers or peers to drive the CALL process.

Accordingly, different authors have focussed their research on SNSLLs (Lamy & Zourou, 2013; Liu et al., 2015), and some have recently focussed specifically on Busuu (Álvarez, 2016; Rosell-Aguilar, 2016; Vesselinov & Grego, 2016). When Busuu migrated to a mobile compatible platform in 2016, it conformed to only three of the eight social aspects identified in SNSs by Boyd and Ellison (2008) and Duffy (2011), namely: create a profile, upload content, and receive feedback. This chapter is centred in the assessment the users made of Busuu as an SNSLL after such a change.

## 2. Methodology

### 2.1. Context and sample

The participants in this study had complete access to the premium version, provided for free by Busuu for research purposes. Following the platform recommendation, the participants were asked to use it daily for a minimum of 10 minutes per day for four weeks, which was the length of the research project. The participants were not asked to fulfil a maximum of hours, as the study tried to reflect the spontaneity of use of other learners.

Using convenience sampling, 268 students from the database of the Worldwise Centre of the University of Central Lancashire were invited via email to take part in this study. Then, using purposive sampling, 14 people were selected: seven (50%) of them had a CEFR A1 level, three (21.42%) A2, two (14.28%) B1, and two (14.28%) B2. That selection led to a diverse group, as Table 1 shows.

Table 1. Generic data of the participants

| Participant | Gender | Age | Nationality | Academic background | Spanish level |
|---|---|---|---|---|---|
| pa01 | F | 49 | British | Graduate | B2 |
| pa02 | F | 20 | British | Undergraduate | A2 |
| pa03 | F | 54 | British | Graduate | A1 |
| pa04 | F | 51 | British | Graduate | A2 |
| pa05 | F | 23 | British | Undergraduate | A2 |
| pa06 | M | 24 | British | Undergraduate | A1 |
| pa07 | M | 47 | British | Graduate | B1 |
| pa08 | M | 23 | British | Undergraduate | A2 |
| pa09 | M | 33 | Belarusian | Graduate | A1 |
| pa10 | F | 18 | British | Undergraduate | A2 |
| pa11 | F | 23 | British | Undergraduate | A2 |
| pa12 | F | 33 | Italian | Graduate | B2 |
| pa13 | M | 44 | British | Graduate | B1 |
| pa14 | F | 21 | Greek | Undergraduate | A2 |

## 2.2. Data collection tools

Based on previous studies that have used similar instruments to evaluate other SNSLLs (Liu et al., 2015), the data collection tools used in this research are presented in Figure 1.

Chapter 4

Figure 1. Data collection tools

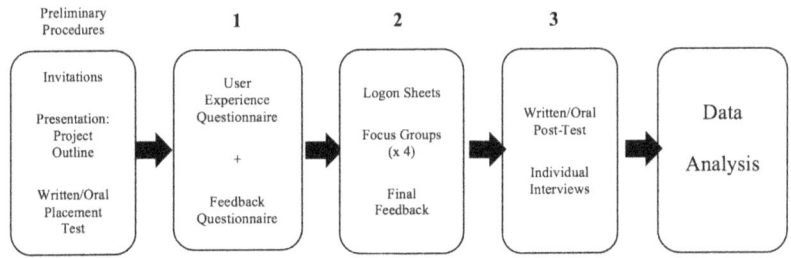

## 3. Discussion of outcomes

As this chapter is focussed on how learners rate Busuu, five different variables obtained from the data collection tools are explored: (1) features that can be found in Busuu; (2) feedback on site design; (3) pre- and post-test results; (4) the social aspect of Busuu; and (5) general perception of the site.

### 3.1. Features that can be found in Busuu

The results obtained via the data collection tools show that learning is not participatory in Busuu. On the contrary, individual learning is encouraged with its current layout, which is counter to a community of practice where learners should share goals and be engaged in continuous collaborative and meaningful activity.

Table 2. Features that can be found in Busuu

| Measurable aspect | 1 | | 2 | | 3 | | 4 | | 5 | |
|---|---|---|---|---|---|---|---|---|---|---|
| | Pre | Post | Pre | Post | Pre | Post | Pre | Post | Pre | Post |
| 1. Creating a profile | 3 | 2 | 6 | 7 | 5 | 1 | 0 | 0 | 0 | 0 |
| 2. Friending | 7 | 6 | 1 | 0 | 5 | 3 | 1 | 0 | 0 | 1 |
| 3. Vocabulary | 6 | 0 | 2 | 0 | 4 | 2 | 2 | 5 | 0 | 2 |
| 4. Posting | 2 | 2 | 2 | 0 | 3 | 2 | 7 | 5 | 0 | 1 |

30

| | | | | | | | | | |
|---|---|---|---|---|---|---|---|---|---|
| 5. Receiving feedback | 4 | 0 | 2 | 1 | 3 | 3 | 3 | 4 | 2 | 2 |
| 6. Giving feedback | 6 | 4 | 2 | 2 | 5 | 3 | 1 | 1 | 0 | 0 |
| 7. Images | 4 | 2 | 3 | 0 | 4 | 2 | 3 | 4 | 0 | 1 |
| 8. Corrections and comments | 4 | 2 | 3 | 1 | 3 | 1 | 3 | 3 | 0 | 1 |

1= Not useful at all, 5= Very useful

As Table 2 shows, the highest division of opinions related to the usefulness of the learning features found in Busuu. When measuring the friending feature, most participants agreed: seven (50%) said that it was not useful at all in the pre-test, which increased to 60% in the post-test. Learning was not considered participatory as learners were not able to share their learning process with other students.

### 3.2. Feedback on site design

Busuu changed their outline and suspended the friending feature when making their platforms compatible with mobile devices. None of the participants could find/accept friends. Therefore, knowledge was individually rather than socially constructed, as there were no peers to create a meaningful learning environment with.

Accordingly, as Table 3 shows, the highest number of very dissatisfied users, ten participants (71.4%), related to the ease of finding contacts. This increases up to 12 (85.7%) if the 'just' dissatisfied replies are included in the pre-test, and it is also the highest variable for dissatisfaction (seven out of ten participants, 70%) for the post-test. Therefore, none of the users expressed satisfaction with this aspect of the site in both cases.

Table 3. Feedback on site design

| Measurable aspect | 1 | | 2 | | 3 | | 4 | | 5 | |
|---|---|---|---|---|---|---|---|---|---|---|
| | Pre | Post | Pre | Post | Pre | Post | Pre | Post | Pre | Post |
| 1. Ease of finding information | 1 | 0 | 4 | 1 | 5 | 4 | 3 | 4 | 1 | 1 |
| 2. Quality of learning activities | 0 | 0 | 2 | 1 | 6 | 3 | 4 | 4 | 2 | 2 |
| 3. Ease of reading texts | 0 | 0 | 0 | 1 | 5 | 2 | 4 | 3 | 5 | 4 |

| | | | | | | | | | |
|---|---|---|---|---|---|---|---|---|---|
| 4. Appearance | 0 | 0 | 0 | 1 | 4 | 2 | 5 | 3 | 5 | 4 |
| 5. Displaying speed | 2 | 0 | 1 | 1 | 2 | 1 | 5 | 1 | 4 | 7 |
| 6. Entertainment value | 0 | 0 | 2 | 1 | 6 | 3 | 5 | 4 | 1 | 2 |
| 7. Overall learning experience | 1 | 0 | 1 | 0 | 6 | 4 | 6 | 5 | 0 | 1 |
| 8. Instructions for activities | 2 | 0 | 7 | 2 | 3 | 3 | 1 | 3 | 1 | 2 |
| 9. Ease of moving around | 3 | 1 | 6 | 2 | 3 | 2 | 1 | 3 | 1 | 2 |
| 10. Ease of finding contacts | 10 | 4 | 2 | 3 | 2 | 2 | 0 | 1 | 0 | 0 |

1= very dissatisfied, 5= very satisfied

### 3.3. Pre- and post-test results

Busuu allows users to merely create a profile, upload user-generated content, and give/receive feedback to/from peers. The latter two features relate to learning development via shared activities; however, those three characteristics mean only 37.5% of the essential features every SNS should have (Boyd & Ellison, 2008; Duffy, 2011). Results in Table 4 show a comparison between the pre- and post-test results, which would confirm that with those features, Busuu currently favours individual learning instead of social learning. Only one participant (7.69%, Participant 11) did not have a positive outcome. Eight (61.54%) out of 13 participants increased their results up to 1 point. Two participants (15.38%) increased by 2 points. Another participant (7.69%) achieved 2.1 points, and the highest score was obtained by Participant 3 (7.69%), 3.1 points.

Table 4. Pre- and post-tests results

| Participant | Pre-written | Post-written | variation | Pre-oral | Post-oral |
|---|---|---|---|---|---|
| pa01 | 6.6 B2 | 6.8 B2 | 0.2 | B2 | B2 |
| pa02 | 2.1 A2 | | | A2 | |
| pa03 | 1.6 A1 | 4.7 B1 | 3.1 | A1 | A1+ |
| pa04 | 3.5 A2 | 4.9 B1 | 1.4 | A2 | A2+ |
| pa05 | 2.0 A2 | 2.4 A2 | 0.4 | A1- | A1 |
| pa06 | 1.4 A1 | 2 | 0.6 | A1- | A1- |
| pa07 | 5.3 B1 | 7.4 | 2.1 | B1 | B1 |
| pa08 | 2.1 A2 | 2.9 A2 | 0.8 | A1 | A1 |

| pa09 | 1.7 A1 | 2.2 A2 | 0.5 | A1 | A1+ |
| pa10 | 3.9 A2 | 4.3 B1 | 0.4 | A2+ | A2+ |
| pa11 | 2.7 A2 | 1.4 A1 | -1.3 | A1 | A1 |
| pa12 | 7.4 B2 | 9.2 C1 | 1.5 | B2+ | C1 |
| pa13 | 4.4 B1 | 5.3 B1 | 0.9 | B1 | B1 |
| pa14 | 3.7 A2 | 4.3 B1 | 0.6 | A1+ | A1+ |

In contrast, the results of the oral tests were not as positive. The evolution in all cases was minimal. None of the participants could advance a complete level, and four out of six participants (66.6%) who stayed on the same oral level, pointed at the lack of native speakers to practise with as the reason for it.

### 3.4. The social aspect of Busuu

Participants did not have the opportunity to achieve useful knowledge through significant activities as Busuu did not provide the opportunities to interact with others. When asked for the reasons why participants would return to the site or why they would recommend it or not, the viewpoints varied between two extremes. One could be synthesised by what Participant 14 said: "It is a great app. Although I can only see it as an additional feature. You still need to speak to people and use books". On the other hand, we could find what Participant 3 affirmed: "This is supposed to be a social network site to help improve my Spanish. I never found anyone ever that I could connect with".

When asked about what they disliked, 12 out of 14 (85.71%) mentioned the difficulty of navigating the site, and six of those 12 (50%) specifically pointed at the impossibility of contacting other users. In the post-trial questionnaire, when asked about what they liked least, six out of nine participants (66.6%) mentioned not being able to find "friends". Five (55.5%) complained about the site not being user-friendly enough, and three (33.3%) about the grammar contents: not sufficient, not clear enough, or difficult to go back to it when needed. Furthermore, eight out of 14 (57.14%) recommended improvements to its social dimension; Participant 12 suggested that "the social aspect of the network should be implemented".

## 3.5. General perception of the site

As learners do not have the opportunity to create a community of learning, it is difficult for users to drive their own process of learning in SNSs. When asked about the likelihood to return to the site on their own (Table 5), in the pre-test, out of 14 total participants, ten (71.4%) declared they would, while two (14.3%) had some doubts, and a further two (14.3%) were neutral. It is important to highlight that none of the participants said that they would not do it; however, this was due to their commitment to take part in the research, as some of them explained. In the post-test, out of ten total participants, those figures decreased to seven participants (70%) saying that they would return, while the other three (30%) had some doubts.

Accordingly, when asked if they would recommend Busuu to other users to learn Spanish (Table 5), in the pre-test, six participants (42.9%) expressed neutrality in their opinion. Interestingly, five participants (35.7%) said they would not do it, and three others (21.4%) affirmed they would. Figures varied in the post-test: six out of ten participants (60%) still declared neutrality, two (20%) said they would not recommend it, and two (20%) agreed with supporting the site.

Table 5. General perception of the site

| Possibilities | 1 | | 2 | | 3 | | 4 | | 5 | |
|---|---|---|---|---|---|---|---|---|---|---|
| | Pre | Post | Pre | Post | Pre | Post | Pre | Post | Pre | Post |
| 1. Return to the site | 0 | 0 | 2 | 0 | 2 | 3 | 7 | 6 | 3 | 1 |
| 2. Recommend the site | 2 | 1 | 3 | 1 | 6 | 6 | 2 | 2 | 1 | 0 |

1= completely disagree, 5= completely agree

## 4. Conclusions

Although this study has a number of limitations, including the small number of participants, it shows that Busuu facilitates only three out of the eight social aspects every SNS should have. Currently, users only can create a profile, upload user-generated content, and receive feedback from other users, which is not enough for networking and practising the four basic skills of a language.

Busuu's status quo is regressive. It contradicts the 21st-century educational paradigm shift concluded by Wang and Vásquez (2012). It has moved backwards from social to cognitive orientation, from participation to an acquisition metaphor, from L2 use to L2 learning. This backwards shift goes against the fundamental attributes of Web 2.0 technology, such as ease of participation, communication, information sharing, and collaboration (Sturm, Kennell, McBride, & Kelly, 2009). To fulfil its potential as an SNSLL, Busuu should re-implement the social aspects it had.

Therefore, the pre- and post-test variation results of this study particularly contradict Vesselinov and Grego's (2016) stance, according to which Busuu users would need 22.5 hours of study to cover the requirements for one college semester of Spanish as a foreign language.

# References

Álvarez, J. A. (2016). Social networking sites for language learning: examining learning theories in nested semiotic spaces. *Signo y Pensamiento, 35*(68), 66-84. https://doi.org/10.11144/Javeriana.syp35-68.snsl

Blattner, G, & Lomicka, L. (2012). Facebook-ing and the social generation: a new era of language learning. *Alsic: médias sociaux et apprentissage des langues : (r) évolution? 15*(1). http://alsic.revues.org/2413

Boyd, D., & Ellison, N. B. (2008). Social Network sites: definition, history, and scholarship. *Journal of Computer-Mediated Communication, 13*(1), 210-230.

Busuu. (n.d). https://www.busuu.com/en/about

Duffy, P. (2011). Facebook or faceblock. Cautionary tales exploring the rise of social networking within tertiary education. In M. Lee & C. McLoughlin (Eds), *Web 2.0-based e-learning: applying social informatics for tertiary teaching* (pp.284-300). IGI Global. https://doi.org/10.4018/978-1-60566-294-7.ch015

Jones, J. F. (2001). CALL and the responsibility of teachers and administrators. *ELT Journal, 55*(4), 360-367.

Lamy, M.-N., & Zourou, K. (Eds). (2013). *Social networking for language education. New language learning and teaching environments*. Palgrave MacMillan.

Lee, J. S. (2006). Exploring the relationship between electronic literacy and heritage language maintenance. *Language Learning & Technology, 10*(2), 93-113.

Lin, C.-H., Warschauer, M., & Blake, R. (2016). Language learning through social networks: perceptions and reality. *Language Learning & Technology, 20*(1), 124–147.

Liu, M., Abe, K., Cao, M. W., Rosse, S., Ok, D. U., Park, J. B., Parrish, C., & Sardegna, V. G. (2015). An analysis of social network websites for language learning: implications for teaching and learning English as a second language. *CALICO Journal, 32*(1), 113-152.

Rosell-Aguilar, F. (2016). *User evaluation of the busuu language learning app*. Presentation. https://www.slideshare.net/FRosellAguilar/user-evaluation-of-the-busuu-language-learning-app

Sturm, M., Kennell, T., McBride, R., & Kelly, M. (2009). The pedagogical implications of Web 2.0. In M. Thomas (Ed.), *Handbook of research on Web 2.0 and second language learning* (pp.367-384). Information Science Reference..

Vesselinov, R., & Grego, J. (2016). *The busuu efficacy study.* https://www.busuu.com/en/it-works/university-study

Wang, S., & Vásquez, C. (2012). Web 2.0 and second language learning: what does the research tell us? *CALICO Journal, 29*(3), 412-430. https://doi.org/10.11139/cj.29.3.412-430

# 5. 'It's a shame that we haven't met earlier!': facilitating a tandem language exchange programme at Queen's University Belfast

## Liang Wang[1]

---

### Abstract

Tandem Language Exchanges[2] (TLE) have been recognised for their pedagogical value in language learning, especially when developing learner autonomy through providing language learning support to each other in a friendly and social learning environment. Unlike many projects which incorporate cross-site practices in a collaborative teaching paradigm, the TLE programme at Queen's University Belfast aims to support all students and staff who wish to practise with a native speaker of the target language on campus via a platform that facilitates searching, interaction, and socialising functions. Drawing on observation, survey results and self-reports, this study reviews the obstacles to active engagement and reports a case study (Chinese-German) to demonstrate how they felt about their practice and participation. The study concludes with some considerations for implementing this TLE approach as a useful opportunity in complementing formal language learning at university level.

**Keywords: tandem language exchange, informal language learning, TLE platform, language partner, social engagement, intercultural exchange.**

---

1. Queen's University Belfast, Belfast, Northern Ireland; liang.wang@qub.ac.uk

2. http://www.qub.ac.uk/lc/LearningSupport/TLE/

**How to cite this chapter:** Wang, L. (2018). 'It's a shame that we haven't met earlier!': facilitating a tandem language exchange programme at Queen's University Belfast. In F. Rosell-Aguilar, T. Beaven, & M. Fuertes Gutiérrez (Eds), *Innovative language teaching and learning at university: integrating informal learning into formal language education* (pp. 37-46). Research-publishing.net. https://doi.org/10.14705/rpnet.2018.22.774

## 1. Introduction

Queen's University Belfast, like many other universities, has placed great importance on its internationalisation agenda with a vision of becoming a "world class international university that supports outstanding students and staff working in world class facilities, conducting leading-edge education and research focussed on the needs of society" (Queen's University Belfast[3]). To this end, a central goal of its education strategy is to "create an educational experience that enriches our students intellectually, socially, and culturally" (Queen's University Belfast[4]).

The Language Centre exists to provide staff and students with courses, resources, and learning support. Its primary mission is to develop students' global citizenship through enhancing their foreign language skills as well as their cultural awareness and sensitivity. The TLE programme is an extra-curricular initiative designed to provide language learners with an enhanced study experience within Queen's multicultural environment.

TLE, at its simplest, refers to reciprocal support and instruction between two learners, each of whom wishes to improve their proficiency in the other's native language (Appel & Mullen, 2000, p. 291; O'Rourke, 2007). Unlike many TLE projects which incorporate class-to-class or partner-to-partner practices in a well-designed teaching paradigm for language learning or intercultural exchange (Batardière & Jeanneau, 2015; O'Rourke, 2007), this TLE programme provided learners with a free online space that relied on the principles of reciprocity and autonomy (Appel & Mullen, 2000; O'Rourke, 2007). That is, TLE participants at Queen's did not have to register with a Language Centre course in order to join in this programme.

---

3. https://www.qub.ac.uk/home/Vision2020/VisionStatement/

4. http://www.qub.ac.uk/teachers/Filestore/Filetoupload,756282,en.pdf

## 2. What we did

Since its pilot implementation in 2015, we created an online registration form to record the language exchange needs and basic personal information of the participants. Invitation letters were then sent out with instructions to create an account for their online participation. The platform, firstly a university-affiliated blog which did not enable participant interactivity well, was later replaced by CANVAS, an online learning space that allows the creation and delivery of self-designed courses. Structured as a course, the TLE platform assembled all necessary resources labelled as modules (work sheets, safety advice, participant stories, etc.) and tools (calendar, inbox) to help participants develop their partnership. In particular, it embedded language-specific discussion forums that enabled participant presence and interaction (see Figure 1).

Figure 1. The participant view of the TLE platform

As soon as participants activated their accounts, they were able to advertise their language exchange needs by both writing in their profiles and identifying their native languages, as shown in Figure 2.

For example, English native-speakers would need to introduce themselves by posting in the English forum, regardless of their target languages. Then, they would need to browse through the other language forums to look for potential

Chapter 5

language partners and vice versa. However, participants were advised not to post their exchange needs directly in a forum of their target language(s) to avoid confusion. This way, they could afford more than one partnership as long as both sides agreed.

Figure 2. Example of setting up a partnership by participants via the discussion forums

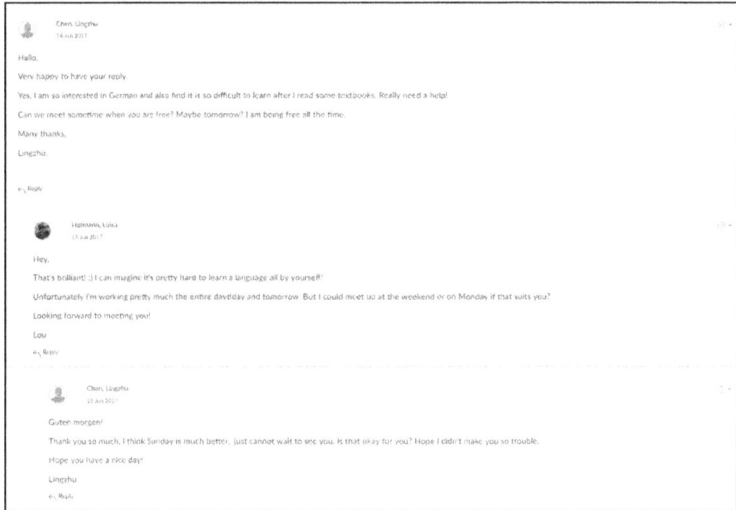

Meetings were scheduled to facilitate the TLE registration and participation throughout the semesters. Usually after the start of the semester, an initial group meeting was arranged to brief the participants, share experiences, and undertake ice-breaking activities, without necessarily partnering with one another on site due to their different availabilities. Monthly meetings were arranged afterwards for on-going support. Updates on TLE activities were circulated by the organiser via announcements in the platform. However, attending the TLE meetings was voluntary. With regard to individual communication, functions such as the inbox and private messages allowed the organiser and participants to email each other. Worksheets (e.g. learning diary template) were also available.

## 3. Method

Data were collected using an end-of-semester survey and through a set of observations; these data were presented with descriptive analyses to frame the subsequent case study. The programme evaluation survey was sent to the 149 participants who registered with the TLE programme. Due to clashes with the exam period and unreported drop-outs, only 18 participants finally returned their feedback (one incomplete), with a response rate of 12.08%. The questions focussed on their experience of using the TLE service and their perceived benefits and drawbacks of TLE participation. The observation data came from their registration with the TLE platform with regard to native language and target language. The analysis of the case was based on the participants' online participation and a series of follow-up emails.

## 4. Discussion of outcomes

### 4.1. The wider context

The survey evaluation revealed that among the 18 respondents, only five had started TLE practice. The rest reported that they had met their partner only once (27.78%) or had not met their partner since joining the programme (44.44%). In all six TLE meetings, only one participant attended three sessions, with ten reporting non attendance. The participants met on average once a week, often in campus areas such as the café or the student lounge. Three main reasons explain the low participation or no participation (Table 1): heavy workload (58.82%), difficulties to agree a time to meet (41.48%), and no suitable partners (29.41%).

This is consistent with reports from similar studies (Batardière & Jeanneau, 2015). Compared to the initial registration number, it is not difficult to see that despite the enthusiasm of registering with the programme, non-credit bearing learning could de-motivate participants and failure to find a suitable time to meet could reduce commitment to each other.

Table 1. Main reasons for low participation or no-participation

| Answer Choices | Responses |
|---|---|
| Heavy workload | 58.82% (10) |
| No suitable partners (not the right level, lack of communication, etc.) | 29.41% (5) |
| Difficult to find an agreed time slot (timetable clashes, etc.) | 41.18% (7) |
| Change in circumstances (illness, placement, etc.) | 5.88% (1) |
| Unsure how to get started | 17.65% (3) |
| Other (please specify) | 11.76% (2) |
| Total respondents | 17 |

In addition, a great imbalance between language exchange demands made it problematic for participants to find their ideal language partners. For example, there existed an overall shortage in supply of languages compared to the demand, except for English and Chinese, as shown in Table 2. It is worth noting that the numbers quantitatively matching both 'native languages' in supply (e.g. Italian) and 'target languages' in demand (e.g. Italian) did not indicate an automatic pairing up.

Table 2. Imbalanced demands in TLE participation

| Native languages | Target languages | Native languages | Target languages |
|---|---|---|---|
| Arabic (1) | Arabic (6) | Korean (1) | Korean (8) |
| Bengali (1) | N/A | Latin (1) | N/A |
| Catalan (1) | N/A | Chinese (27) | Chinese (8) |
| Dutch (1) | Dutch (1) | Polish (1) | Polish (1) |
| French (9) | French (52) | N/A | Portuguese (4) |
| German (3) | German (23) | Russian (1) | Russian (1) |
| Greek (2) | N/A | Spanish (7) | Spanish (64) |
| Irish (1) | Irish (1) | N/A | Swedish (2) |
| Italian (9) | Italian (9) | Turkish (1) | Turkish (1) |
| N/A | Japanese (3) | English (88) | English (39) |

Regardless of the challenges, those participants with a genuine interest in language learning (e.g. 'day-to-day conversation') and intercultural exchange (e.g. 'meet people' and 'understand the culture and the language') managed to start their TLE, as the case below illustrates.

## 4.2. A case report: a tale between two TLEers

Lingzhu, a native Chinese student of pharmacy at Queen's since September 2016, registered with the TLE in June 2017. She was unable to register for a German course because of her tight timetable during term time. When she finished most of her research work in May 2017, she decided to learn some German by herself in order to get 'something useful' out of her time before returning to China. Having no specific plan, she found self-study was really challenging without someone to help her and she turned to the TLE programme for support. After posting a greeting message as advised by the organiser, she was quickly contacted by Luisa the next day (see Figure 2).

Luisa moved from Nuremberg, Germany, to Belfast in October 2016 for a gap year experience and she registered with the TLE in order to find language partners to further improve her already fluent English, basic French, and Spanish. She said that her first few partnerships were all 'rather one-sided' as the native English speakers 'couldn't teach' her English to the extent that she helped them in German. However, she acknowledged the benefits of learning about the cultural aspects of the local area and the UK in general. Through a consultation email, the organiser advised her to keep her target language learning options open for more opportunities. So she did and found Lingzhu quickly.

They arranged their first face-to-face meeting on Sunday the 18th of June after a few exchanges through the forum discussions. They decided to meet up every other day at the library lounge during the morning hours (see Figure 3). They tried to spend equal time on German and Chinese practice as much as possible, although they found themselves getting stuck talking about cultural topics even in English. Luisa described their meetings on language exchange as follows:

> "Although we both use a book [...] we usually don't use them for our meetings. Most of the time we [...] collect words or phrases in the form of mind maps or tables. We have already been very busy with

vegetables, fruits, food, the weather, the seasons and verbs in German and [...] we've done some basic introduction and greeting phrases, numbers, how to draw Chinese signs and how [...] grammar works. Pronunciation also plays a very important role for us and we try to spend as much time talking and reading as possible" (Luisa, email, 14/07/2017).

Figure 3. Lingzhu and Luisa as TLE partners (published with permissions from the participants)

Likewise, Lingzhu appreciated the social value of making friends for intercultural exchange via the TLE programme. She said:

"Every time Luisa and I meet up, we not only learn [languages] from each other, but also talk about the different culture[s] [...] We talk about the life, the food, hobbies and so on. We go out running, do sports together" (Lingzhu, email, 10/07/2017).

Luisa, while initially having no intention to learn Chinese, thanked Lingzhu for her patience in helping with her pronunciation practice and answering 'silly' questions that she would not attempt with a teacher in class. She also felt grateful for the chance of learning about Chinese culture much more than she would learn from a book. Echoing Lingzhu's words, she further valued this TLE partnership and beyond, even using a recently learned expression from the organiser:

> "What started off as a language partnership soon turned into a real friendship and apart from learning [languages] we also [...] spend time as friends. I'm very grateful [...] and I really hope our friendship and language partnership will last for a long time even though I'm back home in Germany over summer and she goes back to China [...] It's a shame we haven't met earlier! 相见恨晚 (xiāngjiàn hènwǎn)" (Luisa, email, 14/07/2017).

## 5. Conclusion

This study indicates that a TLE programme like this could be facilitated for participants with different purposes, from developing language skills to fostering friendships. Despite the limitations of this study in terms of scale and size, it is worth suggesting a couple of points for further development.

The key to an effective operation is two-sided. Firstly, in a loosely organised on-campus learning environment, the organiser's dedication to leading and maintaining an active role is as important as the participants' commitment. A mere exposure of contacts via the TLE platform does not necessarily guarantee any sustainable partnerships. A careful process of facilitation and moderation should be rendered to ensure a meaningful exchange, as seen in Luisa and Lingzhu's case. Secondly, it is fundamental that participants invest their time and energy on top of their enthusiasm.

With regard to its further development from the organiser's point of view, it would be ideal that such a participation be officially recognised with an award on top of the participants' degree study or language programme, with evidence provided by learning diaries, for instance. This would, in fact, suggest a joint effort between student support services and language tutors alike for the implementation, which would likely be the next stage of Queen's TLE programme development.

## References

Appel, C., & Mullen, T. (2000). Pedagogical considerations for a web-based tandem language learning environment. *Computers and Education, 34*(3-4), 291-308. https://doi.org/10.1016/S0360-1315(99)00051-2

Batardière, M. T., & Jeanneau, C. (2015). Facilitating a face-to-face tandem language exchange on a university campus. *Studies in Self-Access Learning Journal, 6*(3), 288-299.

O'Rourke, B. (2007). Models of telecollaboration (1): eTandem. In R. O'Dowd (Ed.), *Online intercultural exchange* (pp. 41-61). Multilingual Matters.

# Section 2.
# Testing and evaluating language learning tools

# 6 ImparApp: Italian language learning with MIT's TaleBlazer mobile app

## Tiziana Cervi-Wilson[1] and Billy Brick[2]

### Abstract

Recent developments in mobile technologies have increased the ways in which languages can be learnt, both within and beyond the classroom. Whereas the use of mobile technologies seems to challenge traditional knowledge and skills acquisition, research shows that foreign language study can be enriched through easy access to resources selected to suit individual interests or needs (Kukulska-Hulme, 2013). This chapter reports on an Italian language learning game, *ImparApp*, developed with the Massachusetts Institute of Technology's (MIT) *TaleBlazer* location-based game-authoring tool. Players interact with virtual characters, objects, and data as they move around their real physical location whilst attempting to solve a time travel mystery. This chapter presents data collected through a case study of how learning a language can take place beyond the traditional classroom in new and challenging ways. The chapter summarises the way learning activities were integrated into the app and discusses how the learning challenges were designed across the scenes, episodes and settings. It also presents data collected from the 'play-test' sessions and discusses initial findings of the pilot project.

Keywords: mobile learning, language learning, gamification, Italian.

1. Coventry University, Coventry, United Kingdom; tiziana.cervi-wilson@coventry.ac.uk

2. Coventry University, Coventry, United Kingdom; billy.brick@coventry.ac.uk

How to cite this chapter: Cervi-Wilson, T., & Brick, B. (2018). ImparApp: Italian language learning with MIT's TaleBlazer mobile app. In F. Rosell-Aguilar, T. Beaven, & M. Fuertes Gutiérrez (Eds), *Innovative language teaching and learning at university: integrating informal learning into formal language education* (pp. 49-58). Research-publishing.net. https://doi.org/10.14705/rpnet.2018.22.775

## 1. Introduction

Recent mobile and web technological developments have allowed for experimentation in the delivery of language learning. Following up on a pre-pilot (Charitonos, Morini, Cervi-Wilson, & Brick, 2016), this chapter presents the initial results of a pilot Italian language learning app, which focusses on a pervasive and game-based approach to teaching and learning within a university context. The app is aimed at students attending an eleven-week Absolute Beginners' module in Italian at Coventry University – Common European Framework of Reference for languages (CEFR) level half of A1. Students move around the Coventry University campus and Coventry city centre while completing tasks and challenges by collecting items for their inventory in order to solve a time travel mystery. Specific tasks are triggered by students' Global Positioning System (GPS) coordinates on their phones, and students and tutors are also able to monitor progress via a leaderboard. By situating games in the real world, mixed-reality and location-based games aim to engage students in an array of experiences that combine real landscapes and other aspects of the physical environment with contextualised digital information supplied to them via mobile devices. The game is divided into four parts, each of which must be completed before players are able to 'level up'.

Authors such as Godwin-Jones (2017) have written extensively about the increasing importance of mobile phones in learners' lives and how they can be utilised for language learning, as the price of data has fallen and the availability of open Wifi networks has increased. In spite of this, Mobile-Assisted Language Learning (MALL) remains "on the fringes" (Burston, 2014, p.115) with behaviouristic type drill and kill activities remaining prominent. Various studies have been carried out into the affordances of some MALL applications, including Rachels and Rockinson-Szapkiw (2018) who demonstrated that students learn as much using *Duolingo* as those in a traditional face-to-face learning environment. A similar study, focussing on the mobile language learning application *Busuu* (Kétyi, 2015) revealed positive outcomes compared to the control group. Another study, Castañeda and Cho (2016), has also demonstrated that integrating a game-like application in a classroom contributed to the improvement of student accuracy and confidence in conjugating Spanish verbs. The cost of creating apps has also fallen and the number of those available, either designed specifically for language learning such as *Duolingo,* or those that can be utilised for this purpose, has increased rapidly. To categorise these, Rosell-Aguilar (2017) presented a taxonomy of available apps and how they could be used for foreign language learning (p. 249). He also presented a framework, consisting of four categories and criteria through which apps can be evaluated.

## 2. The context and the design background

### 2.1. Language learning at Coventry University

Coventry University offers students the opportunity to learn a foreign language by attending an institution-wide language learning programme, 10-credit-bearing 'Add+vantage' module. As well as developing students' foreign language competence, these modules aim to develop and expand students' employability skills.

The purpose of the project was to investigate the interface of game-based learning and pervasive learning in support of language teaching and learning and to evaluate the holistic and modular design model (see Figure 1) as a tool to guide the different layers of the design process, as suggested by Arnab et al. (2015). The pilot study took place in the spring semester of 2016 and the following sections describe this process.

In line with the EU's *Opening up Education* initiative, the team's choice was to use the MIT's *TaleBlazer* (Medlock-Walton, 2012) authoring tool. The prototype game was developed with the MIT augmented reality platform, *TaleBlazer*, which is an open-source authoring tool to facilitate the development of location-based augmented reality games. The game mechanics informed how the students can interact with their physical environment and learn Italian at the same time. The content and learning objectives of the app were aligned to the curriculum of the Beginners Italian modules at Coventry University. The user-centred design and the establishment of a multi-disciplinary team consisting of researchers, tutors, and students were key factors in the development of the app pertaining to educational contexts. Two undergraduate students, one studying English and Creative Writing, and the other Gaming Technologies, wrote the storyline and coded *Taleblazer* respectively. Lecturers provided the expertise in Italian language, culture, pedagogy, and content, whilst the educational technology researchers provided the necessary skills for the development of an educational app.

Figure 1.   Holistic and modular framework (Arnab, 2016)

| Layer 4: Technology | Interfaces | Media | Analytics | Communication | Storage |
|---|---|---|---|---|---|
| Layer 3: Gameful Design | Mechanics | Dynamics | Aesthetics | EX | UX |
| Layer 2: Learning Dynamics | Mode | Location | Activities | Assessment | |
| Layer 1: Learning Context | Learners | Pedagogy | Learning units | KPI | In/non/formal |

The game prompts students to explore the city's buildings and heritage through specifically designed mobile phone tasks, triggered by students' GPS coordinates. These tasks focus on the four language skills of reading, writing, listening, and speaking. Students and tutors are also able to monitor progress via a leaderboard and players are able to compete with each other. The app's design is discussed in Morini et al. (2016), where it is noted that one of the key aspects of the design approach is that it allows its users to experience their everyday living contexts and their course's content "in a new and playful way" (p. 96).

## 2.2.   Learning objectives and content

The learning objectives and content of the *ImparApp* prototype game are wholly aligned to the syllabus of an 11-week Absolute Beginners Italian language module at Coventry University, equivalent to half of the CEFR (Council of Europe, 2001) for languages level A1: Breakthrough. *ImparApp*, in the first instance, aims to supplement classroom activities and to consolidate and deepen students' linguistic competences. Depending on the outcomes of the pilot project, consideration will be given to using *ImparApp* in a blended mode, where students would only attend classes on a bi-weekly basis rather than in full-time mode. In the weeks they do not attend class, they will complete challenges and tasks within the app in self-guided mode. As mentioned in Charitonos et al. (2016, p. 96), through the targeted use of the app, students will have various opportunities to practise speaking and to write short passages using appropriate grammatical structures for the task and the level. Further to this, students should be in a position to recognise information and understand short texts with simple familiar words and phrases about themselves, their family, and concrete situations they know well (Council of Europe, 2001).

The app is divided into four parts. Aspects of the language are introduced gradually to the user. For example, the meta-text in Part 1 is in English while Part 2 makes use of English and includes an Italian translation in brackets (see Figure 2). Part 3 is mostly in Italian and includes translation in English in brackets. Finally, Part 4 is exclusively in the target language. As well as the language, the app also embeds content which aims to raise students' awareness of Italian culture. The game engages the users in a time travel mystery tale. The protagonist, an Italian researcher at Coventry University, decides to hijack a time machine and travels back in time with the intention of making the UK, and specifically Coventry, part of the Italian-speaking Roman Empire. Through the narrative, students have to contextualise the Italian language and culture gradually broadening their linguistic competence and digital fluency. One aspect of the narrative is to prompt users to explore the city by relating fictional, time travel connected tasks about Coventry's history, culture, and built heritage in a playful way. To progress through the game, students are required to carry out increasingly difficult challenges at the game's four levels. Additional points can be earned by completing further exercises focussing on cultural and language topics, hence embedding features that may help students connect incidental and deliberate learning activities (Gaved et al., 2013).

Figure 2. Examples of how the language is introduced

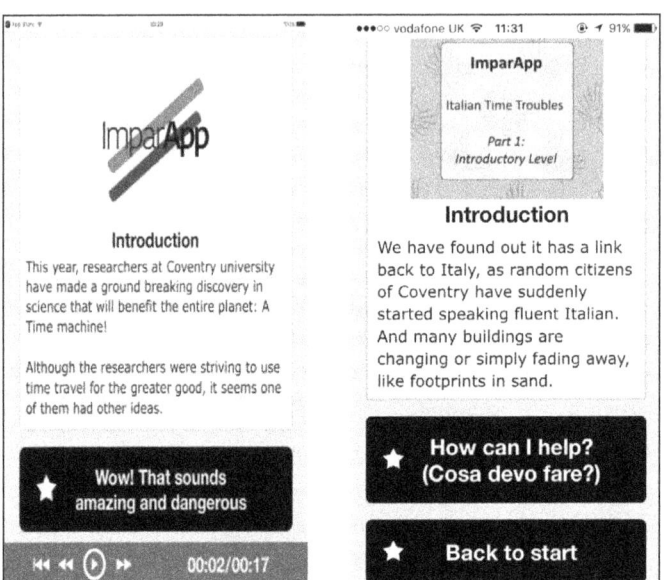

## 3. What we did

The initial 'play-test' session of *ImparApp* was conducted with the intent of providing the team with feedback to progress to further iterations of the game. Data collection was carried out through a series of open-ended oral questions posed to the participants both before and after the 'play-test' session. Initially, students were observed by the researchers using a structured observation sheet, further data were collected via a focus group with participants, tutors, and researchers. Seven students, attending a lower intermediate level Italian language module at Coventry University (CEFR A2), took part in the testing of Part 1 of the game. Part 1 of 4 provides an introduction to the game itself, including a manual which explains in detail the rules and mechanics of the game. This particular cohort was deliberately selected for the pre-pilot play-testing as their knowledge of the Italian language allowed them to focus mainly on the usability and engagement aspects of the game rather than the language itself. Members of the research team accompanied the selected students around Coventry, acting as passive observers and note-takers as they worked their way through the game.

The initial findings of the data collected in the 'play-test' session revealed overwhelmingly positive feedback. Students found the pervasive game-based delivery of content engaging and effective. The data suggested that students were particularly fascinated by the narrative and were curious to find out how it ended. This indicates an interest for the immersive side of the game-based learning experience. In line with Whitton's (2014) study, students also expressed a desire to hear the storyline and instructions as sound effects embedded in the game rather than an over-emphasis on having to read them. Some negative comments were made by the students regarding the language level as being unsuitable for their language competence. As mentioned previously, having some prior knowledge of the language was a key part of the design of the 'play-test' session so that the focus of the students was specifically aimed at the game dynamics rather than the language. Further observations revealed aspects of the game that were not anticipated in the design. These included social and competitive aspects, e.g. competing and racing against the other groups. This manifested itself particularly in a desire for each group to race each other to the next location to further advance in the game. As expected when testing a prototype, other points emerged from this data, but these were mostly of a technical nature, i.e. related to interface and usability (e.g. a desire for a map zoom feature and personal avatar creation). Students' comments (e.g. add audio files) were addressed in the next iteration of the app and as a result, exploration pathways were re-designed to provide a more meaningful itinerary in the city centre. For example, a participant referred to a historic pub in Coventry: "Whitefriars Pub… I didn't know anything about the pub and the little alley behind the cathedral". Finally, in the focus group, discussion participants touched upon issues of assessment. Students shared some concerns and expressed a preference for traditional methods of assessment. For example, a participant said "you can go off the app and do the assessment checking answers on a laptop. So, still, you [teachers] need to do assessment in class".

Examples of incidental learning also emerged from the data, including embedding opportunities for students to interact with each other and with the built environment to avoid the 'heads-down' effect (Hsi, 2003).

## 4. Next steps

As a result of the 'play-test' session and associated iterations of the game, the *ImparApp* project enters its second phase of development, which involves further testing with key stakeholders. For example, a 'blind-test' session of the first four parts of the game will be organised, and a general invitation to students at Coventry University will be distributed. In this phase, users will be encouraged to offer feedback, and contribute to future iterative improvements of game and learning design specifics. In the final phase of the pilot project, on completion of *ImparApp*, full implementation within the Beginners Italian Course at the university, and a wider engagement with potential users will be sought, allowing the research team to inquire into a further level of the potentialities of pervasive, game-based, and mobile learning approaches in the context of foreign language learning and teaching.

## 5. Conclusions

This study was conceived to determine the affordances a gamified approach to language acquisition offered to learners. This went beyond existing studies in so far that learners were required to undertake activities and tasks outside the classroom walls (Charitonos et al., 2016). Depending on the outcomes of the pilot project, consideration will be given to using *ImparApp* in a blended mode, where students would only attend classes on a bi-weekly basis rather than in full-time mode. In the weeks they do not attend class they will complete challenges and tasks within the app in self-guided mode. Through the targeted use of the app, students will have numerous opportunities to practise speaking and to write short passages using appropriate grammatical structures for the task and the level. Further to this, students should be able to recognise information and understand short texts with simple familiar words and phrases about themselves, their family, and concrete situations they know well (Council of Europe, 2001). Initial findings show that the prototype game allows students to experience their everyday living contexts and their module's content in an innovative and fun way. The project has informed the design of future iterations and has prompted the team to rethink some of the design and organisation of the app before it can be fully integrated into the curriculum. Also, Rosell-Aguilar's (2017) framework presents the team with a robust set of criteria against which the app can be evaluated.

## References

Arnab, S., Tombs, G., Duncan, M., Smith, M., & Star, K. (2015). Towards the blending of digital and physical learning contexts with a gamified and pervasive approach. *Proceedings of Games and Learning Alliance (GALA) Conference*, Rome, October 2015.

Arnab, S. (2016, January 2). *A holistic approach to designing gamified and pervasive learning*. https://sylvesterarnab.com/tag/trans-disciplinary/

Burston, J. (2014). The reality of MALL: still on the fringes. *CALICO Journal, 31*(1), 103-125. https://doi.org/10.11139/cj.31.1.103-125

Castañeda, D. A., & Cho, M. (2016). Use of a game-like application on a mobile device to improve accuracy in conjugating Spanish verbs. *Computer Assisted Language Learning, 29*(7), 1195-1204. https://doi.org/10.1080/09588221.2016.1197950

Charitonos, K., Morini, L., Cervi-Wilson, T., & Brick, B. (2016). Urban explorations for language learning: a gamified approach to teaching Italian in a university context. In S. Papadima-Sophocleous, L. Bradley, & S. Thouësny (Eds), *CALL communities and culture – short papers from EUROCALL 2016* (pp. 94-99). Research-publishing.net. https://doi.org/10.14705/rpnet.2016.eurocall2016.544

Council of Europe. (2001). *Common European framework of reference for languages*. Cambridge University Press.

Gaved, M., Kukulska-Hulme, A., Jones, A., Scanlon, E., Dunwell, I., Lameras, P., & Akiki, O. (2013). Creating coherent incidental learning journeys on mobile devices through feedback and progress indicators. In *12th World Conference on Mobile and Contextual Learning (mLearn 2013)*, 22-24 October 2013, Doha, Qatar, QScience.com. https://doi.org/10.5339/qproc.2013.mlearn.13

Godwin-Jones, R. (2017). Smartphones and language learning. *Language Learning & Technology, 21*(2), 3-17. http://llt.msu.edu/issues/june2017/emerging

Hsi, S. (2003). A study of user experiences mediated by nomadic web content in a museum. *Journal of Computer Assisted Learning, 19*(3), 308-319. https://doi.org/10.1046/j.0266-4909.2003.jca_023.x

Kétyi, A. (2015). Practical evaluation of a mobile language learning tool in higher education. In F. Helm, L. Bradley, M. Guarda, & S. Thouësny (Eds), *Critical CALL – Proceedings of the 2015 EUROCALL Conference*, Padova, Italy (pp. 306-311). Research-publishing.net. https://doi.org/10.14705/rpnet.2015.000350

Kukulska-Hulme, A. (2013). *Re-skilling language learners for a mobile world*. The International Research Foundation for English Language Education. http://www.tirfonline.org/wp-content/uploads/2013/11/TIRF_MALL_Papers_Kukulska-Hulme.pdf

Medlock-Walton, M. P. (2012). *TaleBlazer: a platform for creating multiplayer location based games*. Doctoral Thesis, Massachusetts Institute of Technology.

Morini, L., Charitonos, K., Arnab, S. et al. (2016). ImparApp: designing and piloting a game-based approach for language learning. *Proceedings of The European Conference on Games Based Learning 2016, Paisley, Scotland*.

Rachels, J. R., & Rockinson-Szapkiw A. J., (2018). The effects of a mobile gamification app on elementary students' Spanish achievement and self-efficacy. *Computer Assisted Language Learning, 31*(1-2), 72-89, https://doi.org/10.1080/09588221.2017.1382536

Rosell-Aguilar, F. (2017). State of the app: a taxonomy and framework for evaluating language learning mobile applications. *Calico Journal*, 34(2), 243-258.

Whitton, N. (2014). *Digital games and learning: research and theory*. Routledge.

# 7 LipDub: a technology-enhanced language learning project with music

## Kirsten Mericka[1]

### Abstract

This chapter presents a technology-enhanced language learning project that was undertaken with advanced first-year university students of German. The students created a LipDub video, which is a music video that combines lip-synching and audio dubbing and can be filmed on any recording device with a camera. To participate in this group project, the students had to use technology and work collaboratively outside of the classroom. The project also involved language learning since the students had to work on their pronunciation and listening comprehension. The videos were, thereafter, incorporated into a formal language lesson in the university's multi-media centre, where the students completed various language tasks with the videos. The videos differed from standard LipDub videos, but the students' overall feedback, based on written reports, the module evaluation questionnaire, and oral responses, was overwhelmingly positive for both the project and the lesson.

Keywords: project-based and collaborative work, use of technology, autonomous learning, music, pronunciation.

---

1. University of St Andrews, St Andrews, Scotland; klm25@st-andrews.ac.uk

How to cite this chapter: Mericka, K. (2018). LipDub: a technology-enhanced language learning project with music. In F. Rosell-Aguilar, T. Beaven, & M. Fuertes Gutiérrez (Eds), *Innovative language teaching and learning at university: integrating informal learning into formal language education* (pp. 59-65). Research-publishing.net. https://doi.org/10.14705/rpnet.2018.22.776

Chapter 7

## 1. Introduction

This chapter presents a technology-enhanced language learning project carried out with advanced first-year students of German. Over the Independent Learning Week in October 2016, the students of a first-year module were instructed to create a LipDub video. A LipDub is a type of music video that combines lip-synching and audio dubbing. A group of people are filmed lip-synching while listening to a song. Afterwards, the video is edited and the original audio of the song is dubbed over the video. It can be filmed on any recording device with a camera.

LipDub videos can be found all over the world now, with many schools using them for media didactics in particular. Though they are not a new concept, the term only originated in the mid-2000's. Lip-synching, karaoke, and other forms of singing have been around much longer, also in the foreign language classroom. Songs are authentic texts, which can be used to train language skills, teach cultural aspects, and facilitate pronunciation. Rodríguez Cemillán (2014) also writes that music and singing are simply "fun". She lists various activities for the use of songs in language teaching, especially for speaking.

This is not necessarily represented in textbooks. When Badstübner-Kizik (2004) looked at German foreign language textbooks, she noticed that if music was included, the activities would rarely focus on speech production but rather on comprehension. Additionally, she found more classical than modern music included in textbooks. Badstübner-Kizik (2004) goes on to argue that songs support language activities in the classroom, which can provide an authentic glimpse into the foreign culture.

Furthermore, Badstübner-Kizik (2007) explains various functions for music in foreign language teaching, including the support of receptive and productive skills (e.g. written and oral, reading and listening comprehension, and pronunciation), the support of a conscious perception (e.g. creativity, patience), the promotion of reflection (e.g. cooperation, motivation) and the promotion of cultural knowledge (e.g. celebrities such as singers, history).

According to Christiner and Reiterer (2015), there is also a link between singing and speaking as these acts are activated in similar areas of the brain. They both use the vocal motor system, so there is a strong similarity between the production of speech and song. Therefore, the main linguistic aim of this project was working on the pronunciation, which meant shaping the lips the right way for lip-syncing. To make it look real, students had to actually sing loudly while filming, thus pronouncing the words like the singers.

Students also worked on their listening skills because they had to listen very carefully to imitate the sounds of the song. When looking up the lyrics, they used their reading skills and translated parts of (or the whole) song. Further aims were exploring an allegedly "fun" way of engaging with the target language in an informal educational setting, which helped the students get to know each other and spark an interest in music from German-speaking countries. All these aims are reflected in the literature mentioned above.

## 2. Description of the project

The thirty-nine participating students were first-year undergraduates in their first semester at university. Their module consisted of one content lecture, one content tutorial, and two language tutorials per week, with each tutorial group having approximately ten students. It was aimed at advanced students who had already passed Scottish Highers, A Levels, or an equivalent qualification in German before coming to university. Their level of German was B1 on the Common European Framework of Reference for languages (CEFR).

### 2.1. Instructions

General instructions were given to the students in German, while the technical instructions relating to synchronisation were given in English. The students had to form groups of four to six and choose a song approximately two minutes long. Participants were encouraged to find songs they liked, but some suggestions were provided. Everyone had to be in front of the camera at least once. Students could use their phone or any recording device with a camera for filming. As it was a group project, not everyone had to be technologically savvy, as only one person per group needed to know how to complete the technical work.

Additionally, each group had to write a report in German about the work stages of the video production, including when they met, why they chose a particular song, how they prepared filming, what went well, and what did not work well. They could also add any further comments about the project to encourage reflection on the process of filming. The reports would provide data on whether the workload was appropriate. Students had approximately two weeks to finish the project. Although the project was not assessed, the reports and the final videos provided evidence of high student engagement with the task.

## 2.2. Filming procedure

The technology component involved working with a recording device and dubbing the video with the original song. Students did not have to edit the video (or the song). Since they had to plan, organise, and complete the video on their own outside the classroom setting, the project promoted autonomous learning in an informal language learning environment. Students did not ask for help and worked well together, according to the reports. They learned how to work in a team with a common goal, which is an important employability skill. From personal observation, students appeared to be highly motivated because they could choose any song in the target language. When they first heard of the project, they were very excited and immediately started brainstorming possible songs.

## 2.3. Follow-up activities

The videos were incorporated into a formal language lesson in the university's multi-media centre a few days later. This was a fifty-minute class in a room with computers. Each student worked on a computer and got a worksheet in German. They had to complete several language tasks while watching the videos within a time limit. The assembled tasks focussed on various language skills. Sample tasks included making a telephone call about a video, recording a comparison between two videos, chatting online with the other students about another video, filling in gaps, answering questions, and translating lyrics. In addition, students were asked to write a comment about one of the videos in the Moodle forum and respond to one comment.

## 3. Outcomes

The outcomes of this project are based on personal observation of the students in class, talking with them, and reading their reports and their written module evaluation at the end of the semester. From these sources, it has become apparent that the students enjoyed each other's videos and making their own. Due to copyright issues, the videos were not published online, and they were taken down from the school server at the end of the semester. The song selection was slightly surprising as the students chose rather old, well-known songs. All songs were deemed appropriate as they did not have any explicit language or deal with controversial subjects.

Not all groups followed the guidelines carefully, so some videos were not consistent with the definition of a LipDub video. The videos had been edited, some groups even added special effects for transitions and there was almost no movement, which LipDub videos usually have. Furthermore, the students did not always sing loudly, which was part of the instructions. There was no feedback given about the reason, but students may have been too self-conscious to sing loudly in front of their classmates or in public, as a lot of videos were filmed in public spaces. The reports (of different lengths) showed that some groups had minor problems with the video editing software. Even though help was offered, it was not requested.

Although pronunciation was a language focus of this project, no immediate feedback was provided to the students. As the filming took place in an informal and autonomous setting, there was no teacher to correct the students. The aim was to imitate the pronunciation of the song, but only as an exercise.

The bonding between the group members had a positive effect on the dynamics in the classroom, which could be observed without difficulty. Friendships started to form or deepen, and students became more comfortable with each other. They developed their social skills.

## 4. Conclusion

The project and its outcomes correspond with the literature presented in the introduction of this chapter. The students' oral and written feedback was positive for both the project and the lesson. That is not to say that every single student enjoyed the project, but there was no openly negative feedback. Overall, they were motivated by choosing an authentic modern song. It was "fun" for them (Rodríguez Cemillán, 2014, p. 53). There was varied training on all five language skills, e.g. written when they had to write a comment and oral with the imitation of the original singing. The students were creative and cooperative. They also expanded their cultural knowledge when researching the songs and understanding the lyrics as well as the (historical) context (Badstübner-Kizik, 2007). Additionally, they worked on their social skills, e.g. teamwork.

The learning process that the students went through would be an interesting topic for further research on the use of LipDub videos. Another aspect worth exploring would be the students' motivation. Is singing along more of an incentive to practise pronunciation than traditional pronunciation exercises? If so, this would support the case for more use of music in foreign language teaching, particularly focussing on pronunciation.

Through undertaking projects like the one presented here, the LipDub video will become better-known for teaching purposes. Using songs to teach a language or culture is easily applicable and requires little effort for teachers. Teachers should not be afraid to use materials they might not be formally trained with. Testing various methods might also help with the diversity of learners as teachers can accommodate individual needs better.

## References

Badstübner-Kizik, C. (2004). Wortschatzarbeit, Schreiben, Hörverstehen ... und was noch? Anmerkungen zur Rolle von Kunst und Musik im Fremdsprachenunterricht. *ÖDaF Mitteilungen, 1*, 6-19.

Badstübner-Kizik, C. (2007). *Bild- und Musikkunst im Fremdsprachenunterricht*. Peter Lang Verlag.

Christiner, M., & Reiterer, S. M. (2015). A Mozart is not a Pavarotti: singers outperform instrumentalists on foreign accent imitation. *Frontiers in Human Neuroscience, 9*, 482. https://doi.org/10.3389/fnhum.2015.00482

Rodríguez Cemillán, D. (2014). Lieder, die ein Deutschlehrer braucht. *Magazin/Extra, 1*, 53-57.

# 8. Video resources in a flipped language classroom: an experience of using videos to flip a Mandarin teaching module

## Zhiqiong Chen[1]

### Abstract

In this study, the author used the Flipped Classroom (FC) approach in one Mandarin teaching module with three types of self-produced videos as pre-class learning material. These videos covered grammar rules, usage of vocabulary, and explanation of texts. The paper first briefly explains the rationale of using such teaching videos. To investigate students' perceptions of using those teaching videos in FC, their feedback and video-viewing records were collected and discussed. The findings reveal that, although not every student used video materials, those who used them favoured grammar videos. To improve student engagement and interactivity of pre-class activities in FC, the author suggests that some pedagogical interventions could be applied in future FC approaches.

Keywords: flipped classroom, Mandarin, teaching video, student engagement.

## 1. Introduction

To free up more in-class time for student interaction, the author adopted the FC approach in one of her accelerated Mandarin teaching modules, where students were introduced to the learning materials in video format before the class. The FC

---

1. Warwick University, Coventry, United Kingdom; zhiqiong.chen@warwick.ac.uk

**How to cite this chapter:** Chen, Z. (2018). Video resources in a flipped language classroom: an experience of using videos to flip a Mandarin teaching module. In F. Rosell-Aguilar, T. Beaven, & M. Fuertes Gutiérrez (Eds), *Innovative language teaching and learning at university: integrating informal learning into formal language education* (pp. 67-78). Research-publishing.net. https://doi.org/10.14705/rpnet.2018.22.777

approach has been practised in second language teaching and some studies have shown a positive impact on students' academic performance, their motivation, attitude to study, and engagement (Alsowat, 2016; Basal, 2015; Hung, 2015; Hojnacki & Häusler-Gross, 2014 cited in Tseng, Broadstock, & Chen, 2016, p. 18; Webb & Doman, 2016). There has been little discussion on how students perceive pre-class learning materials, especially when it is delivered in video format. The intention of the study was to investigate (1) how the students perceive such learning materials in FC; and (2) based on students' perceptions, what could be adapted in FC to help students during their self-study to prepare them for in-class teaching?

## 2. What I did

### 2.1. Using videos to introduce learning materials

In this study, the author transferred grammar and vocabulary knowledge, together with text explanations, to pre-class students' self-study time with three types of video, namely Grammar Videos (GVs), Vocabulary Videos (VVs), and Text Explanation Videos (TEVs). Video format allows the target language to be presented aurally alongside the written form, which helps to connect the Mandarin written form and the sound, as there is no correlation between them.

All three types of video are used to convey declarative knowledge. Criado (2016) states that foreign language learning can be considered skill learning, and to master a foreign language one needs to gain declarative knowledge, procedural knowledge, and automatised knowledge. She points out that "declarativisation demands explicit teaching on the intricacies of the grammatical features for their noticing and understanding" (Criado, 2016, p. 124).

It is commonly recognised that context-based learning helps second language vocabulary learning (Cohen & Aphek, 1980; Kroll & Curley, 1988; Snow, 2005 cited in Lan, Fang, Legault, & Li, 2015, p. 675). Recognising the role of context in second language learning as a means of consolidating known knowledge, Nassaji (2003) suggests that to teach new words to ESL learners, teachers should spend time identifying, defining, and explaining new words explicitly first. When learning Mandarin vocabulary, Shen (2010) suggests that, whenever possible, visual images, such as pictures and visual actions, should be provided together with verbal explanation.

Therefore, in the author's GV, each new grammar rule was explained verbally in English to ensure understanding; then it was followed by examples which were read out in Mandarin. In each VV, depending on the words, apart from explaining the meaning, some of the following activities were presented: (1) illustrations linked to the meaning of the target word; (2) sentences/short paragraphs containing the target word; (3) comparisons with other vocabulary items which have similar meaning; and (4) explanations of Chinese characters' components. Such design aims to simulate contextual environments. Both GVs and VVs were produced using the online screencast tool, Screencast-O-Matic (S-O-M), based on PowerPoint presentation slides.

The third type of video in this study, TEVs, were used to clarify the meaning of selected parts of the textbook where students tended to have queries. The online tool EDpuzzle was used to insert aural explanations into the existing online videos in which native speakers acted out text conversations in natural settings. While listening to authentic conversations, students can hear some grammatical clarifications which aim to help their understanding.

Moodle was used as the delivery platform. Ten students who enrolled into this Mandarin module were involved in this study. Although the students had been learning Mandarin for at least one year, it was the first time they had experienced FC. The FC approach started at the beginning of the academic year and lasted two terms until the end of the module. The module had in-class teaching twice a week, on Tuesdays and Fridays. Each new set of video materials were assigned to students for self-study three days ahead of in-class teaching. Each student also had the textbook from which all the video teaching materials were based.

## 2.2. Data collection

To understand students' perceptions of video teaching, both quantitative and qualitative data were collected via two methods: an end of module teaching questionnaire survey and the online video view records. Nine students out of ten who studied this module completed the survey, seven anonymously. Due to time limitations, there were no follow-up interviews. The questionnaire contains both open-ended and closed questions. In the questionnaires, participants were asked to list their understanding of both the advantages and disadvantages of each type of video. Table 1 shows students' views.

Table 1. Advantages and disadvantages of each type of video: students' views

| | **Advantages:** | **Disadvantages:** |
|---|---|---|
| Teaching grammar with videos | Be prepared before going to the lesson (with questions to ask) Can go back and make revision easier Go into details (more than the textbook) Spend class time to consolidate knowledge, ask questions Easier to absorb | No interaction with the teacher |
| Teaching vocabulary with videos | Learn correct pronunciation (need to read and write by oneself to memorise) Pictures, stories provided in videos assisted in learning and understanding Visuals and explanation help to remember words more easily Explain some meanings linked to other words | No interaction with the teacher Not personal learning style, prefer learning independently Drilling vocabulary has to be a personal task Not good for learning characters |
| Teaching texts with videos | Easy to relate to when watching texts being acted out with explanations straight after it Breaking down the video dialogue which is very fast Understand the texts better Draw attention to certain points which students wouldn't have thought to be problems | Should read/listen to the dialogues without interruption Some of the explanations are covered in the textbook |

Eight out of nine participants listed various advantages with no disadvantages to GVs. One participant didn't think videos could replace the interaction of the teacher with the students; for her, for learning to take place and be memorable, it needed to be active. From her point of view, watching GVs and VVs at home is *solitary* and *passive*. Therefore, she didn't use both types of videos. In contrast to the number of positive respondents on GVs, only four participants thought VV useful. Among the other five participants, apart from the one who thought it was not interactive, the common belief was that vocabulary learning is a personal matter, not something that could be taught by videos. Regarding TEVs, seven out of nine participants felt they were helpful with different advantages, including the participant who did not watch GVs and VVs.

In the questionnaire survey, all the participants were also asked to choose when and how they watched each type of video from the following given categories: before the teaching, after the teaching, before the exams, or at any time when needed; watching each video with or without partially skipping the content. The retrospectively collected data which reflects what students normally did are shown in Figure 1 and Figure 2.

Figure 1. When the participants watched each type of video

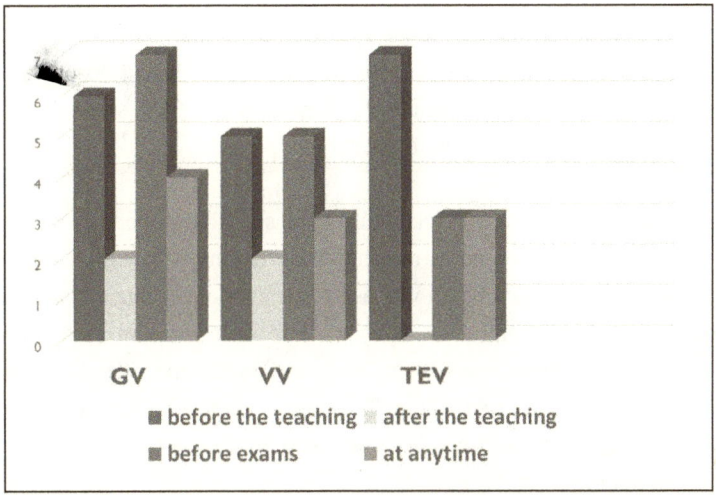

Figure 2. How the participants watched each type of video

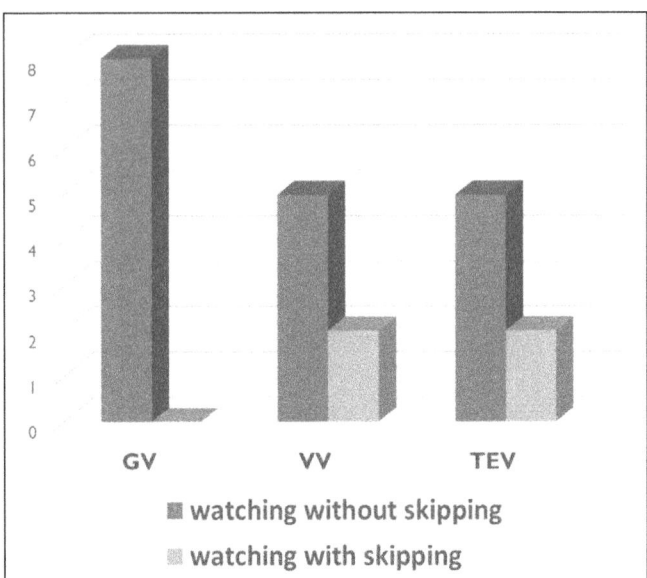

Figure 1 and Figure 2 above show that most of the participants watched GVs before the in-class teaching and before exams without skipping. Similarly, VVs were watched mainly before the in-class teaching and before exams but by fewer participants. Some of them skipped part of the video while watching. TEVs were mostly watched before the in-class teaching and no one watched them immediately after the teaching. With regards to TEVs, some participants skipped sections of the videos while watching them.

Participants were also asked to tick the listed reasons that stopped them watching teaching videos with the choice to add their own reasons. One participant claimed that he/she had been watching all videos in the module teaching and another one did not like learning through GVs and VVs. The other seven all chose *having no time*. Among these seven, one of them also mentioned some videos were too fast to catch and VVs did not really help. The other student who had better listening skills mentioned TEVs did not help, as he preferred watching conversations without any interruption.

In addition to the questionnaire, the number of views of each video was tracked online through S-O-M and EDpuzzle. The following chart shows a section of the view numbers of some videos during the whole module teaching – the rest of the videos were also used by some other students for a different purpose.

Figure 3. Number of views of each video

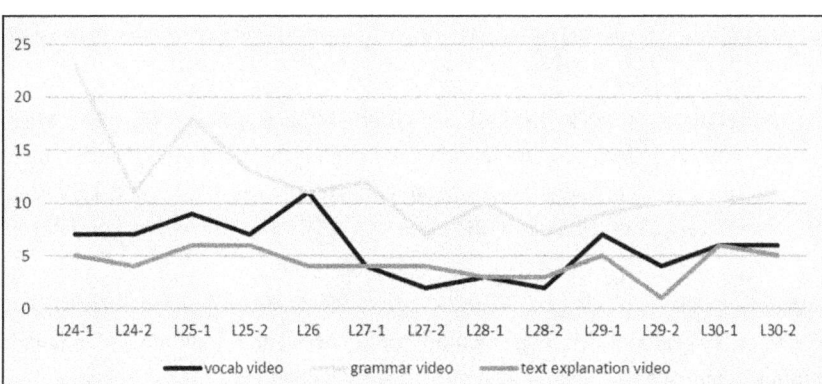

Figure 3 shows that not everyone watched each video. Due to the limited functionality, S-O-M can only record the number of views rather than who watched which videos. For example, if someone watched the same video twice at different times, S-O-M will record two views. However, Figure 3 indicates that GVs were watched repeatedly most of the time. Compared with GVs, VVs have much fewer views, and ten out of the 13 videos were not watched by everyone. Since EDpuzzle can record each user's watching progress, the above chart shows that fewer than six participants watched all the TEVs.

## 3. Discussion of outcomes

Among the three types of video, the data indicate that:

- participants gave most prominence to GVs. It suggests that using video to teach grammar rules is thought to be beneficial and needed. This supports the claim of Criado (2016) and Webb and Doman (2016) that grammatical rules need explicit input;

- all three types of videos were not used just for pre-class self-study, but for revision, consolidation, or clarification purposes. This, to some extent, echoes the advantages of the FC approach in that it increases the retention of materials and allows students to learn at their own pace (Correa, 2015); and

- students watched videos selectively and not everyone used video materials for pre-class learning, which has not been mentioned in most FC research. Even though being considered useful, VVs and TEVs had fewer views, especially the latter.

Apart from personal reasons affecting participants' use of videos, such as time constraints, personal learning method preferences, and individual's language proficiencies, two participants also mentioned VVs and TEVs as not being helpful. Also, comments like *solitary* and *passive* in video teaching should not be ignored. Together with the fact that not everyone used video materials, the negative feedback indicated a need to make pre-class learning materials more engaging.

As the producer, the author could enhance the video design by making it more engaging and interactive. Bergmann and Sams (2012) suggest that instead of one teacher talking in his/her own videos, there could be a pair having conversations. Therefore, more than one perspective could be provided in videos. In addition, more advanced technology/software could be applied for delivering learning materials, for example a 3D Visual Environment (VE) in which students could be engaged through integration of sensory, motor, and action-based information. Lan et al. (2015) used Second Life as the platform in learning Chinese vocabulary and found that 3D VE contexts might enhance vocabulary acquisition which simulates immersive context. Moreover, playing digital video games also helps students retain vocabulary for a longer time (Ebrahimzadeh & Alavi, 2017). However, financial constraints would make it difficult for the author to make such adjustments and inevitably increase the upfront financial investment. It is more feasible to adapt the learning design through pedagogical interventions, which do not involve costly technical adaptations. Thus, the following improvements could be considered.

First, to create a 'need to learn' before directing students to the teaching videos. For example, to design some online quizzes or questions for students to try with their current knowledge. Failure to complete such tasks could become an incentive for them to seek answers from teaching materials, either in video form or from other resources. This might further result in better understanding, as the 'productive failure' process also provides the opportunity for students to understand their own weaknesses, and then focus on some particular parts of the learning materials according to their needs. In this way, learning becomes more individually centred. With the online quizzes, feedback could also be added. If students use them again after self-study, they will be able to check their own progress and have a sense of achievement. O'Flaherty and Phillips (2015) point out that failure to provide formative feedback could cause less engagement with pre-class activity. Both 'need to learn' and getting feedback are fundamental in the learning process.

Second, to encourage learners to take notes while watching instructional videos. The benefit of taking notes in FC has been mentioned in different studies (Bergmann & Sams, 2012; Correa, 2015; Moran & Young, 2015; Muldrow, 2013; Tseng et al., 2016) and its importance in a successful FC has been addressed (Muldrow 2013; Tseng et al., 2016). With note-taking, students can undertake the learning in a reflective manner which could result in consciously engaging with learning materials.

Third, to create decontextualised practise to help vocabulary learning. To accommodate students' vocabulary learning needs and to correspond to the special orthography of Mandarin characters which require repetition to memorise the form and the sound, some decontextualised activities should be introduced alongside VVs to input vocabulary in various ways. Such activities could be online flashcards or picture-word matching activities. At the same time, there is also a need to foster students' awareness of context-based vocabulary learning.

Fourth, to reconsider the usage of TEVs. Instead of assigning such videos, a series of questions could be given out to check students' comprehension. These TEVs could then be used by weaker students who need further clarification.

## 4. Conclusion

This study has provided a snapshot of students' perceptions of using three different types of teaching videos for self-study in a flipped Mandarin teaching module. Due to the small sample and limited data, the results might not be representative. However, the study shows although not every student used teaching videos for self-study, those who used them favoured GVs. To prepare students for in-class teaching in FC, it suggests that attention is needed in engaging students in pre-class learning materials. Consideration should be given to emphasising pedagogical intervention when financial constraints exist, which is the general issue that higher education institutions are currently facing. The next study should investigate the effectiveness of such interventions.

## References

Alsowat, H. (2016). An EFL flipped classroom teching model: effects on english language higher-order thinking skills, student engagement and satisfaction. *Journal of Education and Practice,* 7(9), 108-120.

Basal, A. (2015). The implementation of a flipped classroom in foreign langauge teaching. *Turkish Online Journal of Distance Education,* 16(4), 28-37.

Bergmann, J., & Sams, A. (2012). How to implement the flipped classroom. In J. Bergmann & A. Sams (Eds), *Flip your classroom.* International Society for Tech in Ed. ProQuest Ebook Central.

Cohen, A.D., & Aphek, E. (1980). Retention of second language vocabulary over time: investigating the role of mnemonic associations. *System,* 8(3), 221-235.

Correa, M. (2015). Flipping the foreign language classroom and critical pedagogies: a (new) old trend. *Higher Education for the Future,* 2(2), 114-125. https://doi.org/10.1177/2347631115584122

Criado, R. (2016). Insights from skill acquisition theory for grammar activity sequencing and design in foreign language teaching. *Innovation in Language Learning and Teaching, 10*(2), 121-132. https://doi.org/10.1080/17501229.2015.1090996

Ebrahimzadeh, M., & Alavi, S. (2017). Reader, player, and watchers: short and long-term vocabulary retention through digital video games. *International Journal of Applied Linguistics and English Literature, 6*(4), 52-62. https://doi.org/10.7575/aiac.ijalel.v.6n.4p.52

Hojnacki, S., & Häusler-Gross, K. (2014). *One flipped year in the German program: a story in VII Acts*. American Council on the Teaching of Foreign Languages Conference. 21-23 Nov, 2014, San Antonio.

Hung, H.-T. (2015). Flipping the classroom for English langauge learners to forster active learning. *Computer Assisted Language Learning, 28*(1), 81-96. https://doi.org/10.1080/09588221.2014.967701

Kroll, J. F., & Curley, J. (1988). Lexical memory in novice bilinguals. The role of concepts in retrieving second language words. In M. Grunenberg, P. Morris, & R. Sykes (Eds), *Practical aspects of memory* (2nd ed., pp. 389-395). Wiley.

Lan. Y. J., Fang. S. Y., Legault. J., & Li., P. (2015). Second language acquisition of Mandarin Chinese vocabulary: context of learning effects. *Educational Technology Research and Development, 63*(5), 671-690. https://doi.org/10.1007/s11423-015-9380-y

Moran, C. M., & Young, C. A. (2015). Questions to consider before flipping. *Kappan, Oct.*, 42-46. https://doi.org/10.1177/0031721715610090

Muldrow, K. (2013). A new approach to language instruction-flipping the classroom. *The Language Educator, Nov.*, 28-31.

Nassaji, H. (2003). L2 Vocabulary learning from context: strategies, knowledge sources, and their relationship with success in l2 lexical inferencing. *TESOL Quarterly, 37*(4), 645-670. https://doi.org/10.2307/3588216

O'Flaherty, J., & Phillips, C. (2015). The use of flipped classrooms in higher education: a scoping review. *Internet and Higher Education, 25*, 85-95. https://doi.org/10.1016/j.iheduc.2015.02.002

Shen, H. H. (2010). Imagery and Verbal Coding Approaches in Chinese Vocabulary Instruction. *Language Teaching Research, 14*(4), 485-499. https://doi.org/10.1177/1362168810375370

Snow, M. A. (2005). A model of academic literacy for integrated language and content instruction. In E. Hinkel (Ed.), *Handbook of research in second language teaching and learning* (pp. 693-712). Lawrence Erlbaum.

Tseng, M. F., Broadstock, M., & Chen, H. (2016). An investigation of the design of a four-stage flipped classroom in Mandarin Chinese. *Journey of Technology and Chinese Language Teaching, 7*(1), 15-42.

Webb, M., & Doman, E. (2016). Does the flipped classroom lead to increased gains on learning outcomes in ESL/EFL contexts? *The CATESOL Journal, 28*(1), 39-67.

# 9 The Better French Living Project: how to encourage linguistic, practical, and cultural year-abroad preparation outside the classroom

Sandra Salin[1]

## Abstract

This chapter presents the *Better French Living Project* (BFLP), which was started in 2014 in the French section of the Newcastle University School of Modern Languages (SML) with a view to respond to second-year students' feedback, promote independent learning amongst them, and assist in their year-abroad preparation by developing their practical and intercultural knowledge and listening skills outside the classroom. After introducing the context in which the project was developed, this chapter presents the topics selected, together with samples of the activities that were designed and made available to students via their Virtual Learning Environment (VLE). This is followed by an analysis of the feedback students provided via end-of-year questionnaires in the three academic years from 2014 to 2017, including an assessment of the activities offered and the students' engagement with them. Finally, this chapter suggests how this project could be further developed.

Keywords: year abroad preparation, independent learning, listening skills.

---

1. Newcastle University, Newcastle upon Tyne, United Kingdom; sandra.salin@newcastle.ac.uk

**How to cite this chapter:** Salin, S. (2018). The Better French Living Project: how to encourage linguistic, practical, and cultural year-abroad preparation outside the classroom. In F. Rosell-Aguilar, T. Beaven, & M. Fuertes Gutiérrez (Eds), *Innovative language teaching and learning at university: integrating informal learning into formal language education* (pp. 79-88). Research-publishing.net. https://doi.org/10.14705/rpnet.2018.22.778

Chapter 9

## 1. Introduction

Three main factors contributed to defining the areas the BFLP should focus on. I derived inspiration from my role as Year Abroad Officer for Francophone countries from direct consultation with final-year students and from my knowledge of the second-year language module. This helped me identify what students found particularly challenging, if not overwhelming, while abroad. As module leader, I was also fully aware of the need to develop year-abroad related material that could address gaps existing in the curriculum, including informal register and practical, everyday life situations.

I gave priority to activities related to France because the vast majority of students going to a francophone country during their year abroad choose France as their destination. I focussed on listening activities because understanding native speakers when they speak spontaneously is usually what my students find most difficult to both understand and practise independently. Exposure to the spoken language also offers more opportunities to practise informal register, respects the way we learn a language naturally, and facilitates the development of other skills (Vandergrift, 1999).

## 2. Presentation of the project

Once the main objectives of the project were defined, existing literature in the fields of emotional and cultural intelligence, cultural shock, and adaptation was reviewed in order to better understand the importance and ways of facilitating the transition into the year abroad (Salin, 2017, pp. 172-178). Shanwal and Kaur (2008), for instance, have shown the extent to which emotions and emotional intelligence can affect learning, thus supporting the idea that developing awareness of challenges and exploring ways of tackling them can smooth the transition and contribute to deeper learning.

Dealing with practical, everyday life challenges, like securing accommodation or opening a bank account, may appear somewhat trivial in academic settings.

However, based on my year-abroad students' comments, these practicalities constitute challenges that deeply affect their experience and often make them feel that they are thrown in at the deep end, especially in the first few weeks, all the more so because they feel they have to face them on their own. Thus, addressing these practical aspects – that Winkelman (1994) called *fundamentals* – before students go abroad aimed to facilitate their transition and adaptation:

> "Successful adjustment […] depends on the availability of transition resources necessary for comfortable adaptation in the new culture. The needs of physical well-being, food and security, must be effectively met if one is to […] address subsequent needs for social relations, self-esteem, and personal development. Assistance in managing fundamentals such as food, housing, and transportation then frees the individual to focus on the cultural adaptation issues" (p. 124).

The positive link between preparation and experience is well established and has resulted in new approaches to better prepare students for their placements abroad. For instance, collaborative projects such as the ICP[2] (1997-2000) and the IEREST[3] (2012-2015) projects led to the creation of online resources aiming to develop intercultural awareness. Intercultural Communication is also at the heart of the more recent training programme that López-Rocha and Vailes (2017) offer at the University of Bristol.

The BFLP reflects a different approach in the sense that it adopted independent learning material as a means to better prepare students both culturally and linguistically. This choice was determined by two main factors, the first one being the constraints imposed by the second-year language module, which includes students who do not need to prepare for a year abroad in France (either because they already have undertaken their year abroad or because they will not go there during their year abroad). Additionally, I considered promoting independent learning as a way of encouraging students to move away from

---

2. The Interculture Project: http://www.lancaster.ac.uk/users/interculture/about.htm

3. Intercultural Education Resources for Erasmus Students and their Teachers: http://www.ierest-project.eu/the-project.html

institutional learning into their year-abroad experience where most of their learning would be experiential.

Based on feedback received from year-abroad and final-year students, the following topics were given priority and formed the basic structure of the project material:

- keeping informed about current affairs;
- cultural differences and stereotypes;
- accommodation;
- formal and informal register;
- daily life and socialising;
- banking;
- secondary and higher education;
- applications and interviews; and
- phone conversations.

Reviewing existing online audio-visual resources revealed a lack of sites that matched the language level required and provided in the same package a mix of registers, year-abroad-related topics, and tasks to complete independently, hence the need to design material addressing our students' specificities.

Most of the activities were designed by an intern, Morgane Mazan, a French Postgraduate student undertaking a Master of Arts in Teaching French as a Foreign Language at the University of Nantes. She was almost the same age as our students and had completed a year abroad herself. The BFLP also matched exactly her experience and the topic she had chosen for her dissertation (Mazan, 2014).

According to Reinders (2010), independent learning is more likely to be successful if students receive clear guidance, instructions, answers, and, even better, prompts to help them reflect on their learning. To that end, Mazan (2014) selected 27 online and homemade audio-visual pieces and prepared guided activities, transcriptions, and answer sheets based on them to allow students to work completely independently outside the classroom. She also designed a series of questions and prompts to encourage students to reflect on their own learning and learning styles, what they found difficult, and what steps they could take to improve or overcome these difficulties.

Knowing that even when provided with this kind of support, students still tend to use the material available to them selectively depending on their needs (Reinders, 2010), a pick and mix approach was adopted for the BFLP. Thus, the activities were divided into nine independent units, each corresponding to the above topics, to allow students to focus their independent work on their personal needs and interests.

Although it is not in the remit of this chapter to describe all the material in detail (Mazan, 2014, pp. 89-91, 108-109), it seems relevant to present carefully selected examples to illustrate the pedagogical approach that was applied and the diversity of the areas the students were encouraged to practise.

Some of the audio-visual pieces were selected mainly for their informative nature, but students were still invited to take this opportunity to work on grammar and aspects of spoken French. For example, Mazan used the recorded interview of her French bank manager explaining how to open a bank account to introduce the main banks found in France and key terms related to banking. The transcription was also used to ask students to identify different characteristics of spoken French such as the speech markers *voilà*, *ben*, *hein*, *quoi*, contractions, and grammatical inaccuracies. This activity was also intended to make them aware of the frequency of unfinished sentences and interruptions in a French conversation (Supplementary materials, part 1).

Other pieces were chosen to develop students' cultural knowledge and awareness more specifically, like those contained in the 'Cultural differences and stereotypes' unit that includes three videos exploring how the French are perceived by American, Belgian, and English people. However, developing emotional intelligence was also on the agenda. For instance, two videos featuring

Cyprien, a famous French blogger, podcaster and YouTuber, were used to show the main differences between French and English school lives and education systems, but also to prompt students to think about how feelings and emotions are expressed through tones and body language and how these can vary between countries (Cyprien, 2013, 2015).

As mentioned previously, the characteristics of informal, spoken French, as opposed to academic French, was an important aspect of the BFLP, so the unit on formal and informal languages is not the only one offering students the opportunity to work on slang, colloquial expressions, or speed of delivery. Yet, when Norman, another famous YouTuber, Cyprien, and others appear, this is also to cover very practical topics relevant to everyday life like flat sharing, likes and dislikes, reasons for being late, food shopping, or work-related situations.

## 3. Student evaluation

Students were able to access the material from the first semester of 2014-15 via Blackboard. They were left to use it completely independently in order to assess the extent to which this would enable them to take charge of their year-abroad preparation, in the same way as they would be in charge of their own learning during their year abroad.

In the first year of this project, 2014-15, 87 students were enrolled in the course. At the end of Semester 2, students were asked to complete a questionnaire during their last language seminar, including six questions (Supplementary materials, part 2) aiming to assess their use and experience of the project material in particular. Completion was voluntary. In total, 76 students (87.3% of the cohort) completed it and agreed for their answers to be used for research purposes. Thirty-two respondents (42.1 %) said that they had used the material. In the following year, 85 students were enrolled, followed by 107 in 2016-17. In an attempt to increase the proportion of students using the material, in 2015-16 I included some of the activities into the language module curriculum as independent homework to complement class content. This explains why the proportion of users almost doubled compared to the previous year, as illustrated in Table 1. Looking at actual figures reveals that 50 respondents used the materials in 2015-16 and 56 in 2016-17.

Table 1. Proportion of respondents who used the BFLP material

| 2014-15 (out of 76 respondents – 87.3% of the cohort) | 2015-16 (out of 60 respondents – 70.5% of the cohort) | 2016-17 (out of 64 respondents – 59.8% of the cohort) |
|---|---|---|
| 42.1% | 83.3% | 87.5% |

Additional questions were added to the questionnaire to assess how many students had used the material without being prompted in 2015-16 and 2016-17 (Supplementary materials, part 3). The results, 29 (43.3%) and 28 (43.7%) students respectively, showed that integrating some of the material into the curriculum did not lead to a significant increase in the number of students using the material without being prompted.

Figure 1 presents the top ten aspects that students liked about the material in 2014-15, 2015-16, and 2016-17, based on the 131 students who named up to three things over the whole period. *Preparation for the year abroad*, the original motivation behind the project, was what the students liked most often. Students also acknowledged its usefulness in terms of cultural preparation and language practice. As these two aspects and their constant interaction are important characteristics of what constitutes the year-abroad experience, it can be concluded that the BFLP succeeded in making students *feel* more prepared, if not actually preparing them better.

Out of 140 students who evaluated the BFLP experience in terms of quality and usefulness, 131 found the project good, very good, or excellent between 2014 and 2017. Although integrating some of the material into the language module curriculum allowed me to introduce more year-abroad preparation without taking any additional class time, this also led to a slight drop in the students' positive rating. This would tend to indicate that students are more likely to appreciate the material when they are left to use it independently. Given that not all students on the module will go and spend a year abroad in a francophone country because of the structure of our programmes, this also confirms a link existing between the students' satisfaction and how relevant the material is to them.

Figure 1. Aspects students liked the most

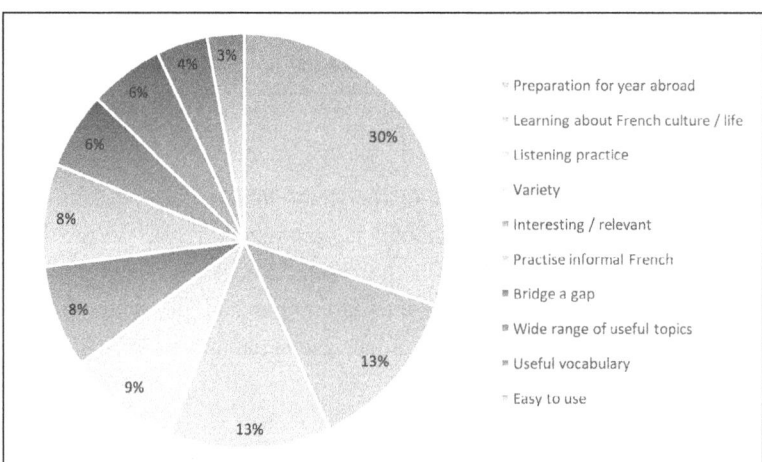

As shown in Table 2, *lack of time* was the most common reason provided by the students who explained why they did not use the material, even when prompted, over the three years. The other reasons found more than once were personal choice, year abroad destination, and the fact that they had already undertaken their year abroad. The 2014-15 results confirm the need to consider time constraints when developing any extra-curricular activities, while the 2015-17 percentages seem to indicate that independent learning is considered as competing with other priorities such as deadlines, assessments, and the workload of other modules, as attested by comments left by students.

Table 2. Proportion of respondents who mentioned *lack of time* as a reason for not engaging with the BFLP material

| 2014-15 (out of 24 respondents) | 2015-16 (out of 27 respondents) | 2016-17 (out of 27 respondents) |
|---|---|---|
| 41.6% | 33% | 38.1% |

## 4. Conclusion

The BFLP can be regarded as successful since students who engaged with it felt more prepared before embarking on their year abroad. Yet, integrating some of its content in the second-year curriculum did not lead to a significant increase in the number of students adopting it as a regular self-selected learning method, which confirms Reinders's (2010) findings.

Although student feedback gave a clear indication of the usefulness of the project before going abroad, further investigation amongst returning students would be needed to evaluate the extent and the kind of impact it had on their year-abroad experience. This could potentially lead to a better understanding of the significance of emotions and feelings, such as enjoyment or confidence, in their learning journey.

A recent survey amongst final-year students has revealed a growing interest in other francophone countries or regions, such as Belgium, Switzerland, and Quebec. The BFLP could be the perfect platform to respond to this kind of demand by offering activities related to these areas. As the project material is now available to all Newcastle University students via the University Internet Protocol TV system, such a development could benefit all students – not just SML students – wishing to go and study or work in a francophone country as part of their degrees. This would go well with the fact that all Newcastle University students are now allowed to undertake a placement year in the UK or abroad as part of their studies.

## Supplementary materials

https://research-publishing.box.com/s/lwqciretknlcd5n2vstaeqio1jr0wjed

## References

Cyprien. (2013). *L'école*. YouTube. http://www.youtube.com/watch?v=RL7grUEo960

Cyprien. (2015). *Mentions Bac*. Dailymotion. http://www.bing.com/videos/search?q=Cyprie n+mentions+Bac&view=detail&mid=439FE41655298423D0B4439FE41655298423D0 B4&FORM=VIRE

López-Rocha, S., & Vailes, F. (2017). Developing intercultural communicative competence for the year abroad experience. In C. Álvarez-Mayo, A. Gallagher-Brett & F. Michel (Eds), *Innovative language teaching and learning at university: enhancing employability* (pp. 67-75). Research-publishing.net. https://doi.org/10.14705/rpnet.2017.innoconf2016.656

Mazan, M. (2014). *Comment sensibiliser des étudiants de l'université de Newcastle à la compétence de compréhension orale du français parlé : mise en place d'un dispositif d'auto apprentissage semi-guidé*. Unpublished MA Dissertation. Université de Nantes.

Reinders, H. (2010). Towards a classroom pedagogy for learner autonomy: a framework of independent language learning skills. *Australian Journal of Teachers Education, 35*(5), 40-55. https://doi.org/10.14221/ajte.2010v35n5.4

Salin, S. (2017). The Better French Living Project: preparing students for 'difference' in France. In R. Whittle & S. Salin (Eds), *Preparing modern languages students for 'difference'* (pp. 169-198). Peter Lang.

Shanwal, V. K., & Kaur, G. (2008). Emotional intelligence in education: applications and implications. In: R. J. Emmerling, V. K. Shanwal, & M. K. Mandal (Eds), *Emotional intelligence: theoretical and cultural perspectives* (pp. 153-170). Nova.

Vandergrift, L. (1999). Facilitating second language listening comprehension: acquiring successful strategies. *ELT Journal, 53*(3), 168-176. https://doi.org/10.1093/elt/53.3.168

Winkelman, M. (1994). Cultural shock and adaptation. *Journal of Counselling and Development, 73*(2), 121-126. https://doi.org/10.1002/j.1556-6676.1994.tb01723.x

# 10 Multimodal Corpus of Spanish Speech Acts: main features and potential pedagogical uses

## Marta Vacas Matos[1]

### Abstract

Most of the more serious mistakes we make in our second or third languages are not linked to grammar, but to pragmatics (Félix-Brasdefer, 2008; Kasper & Rose, 1999; Olshtain & Blum-Kulka, 1985; Rose & Kasper, 2001). While language textbooks are often focused on grammar content distributed throughout a communicative syllabus (Lázaro Ruiz, 2014; Lörscher & Rainer Schulze, 1988), students are still missing the pragmatic rules that are behind the behaviors of native speakers and their use of language. This chapter talks about the creation and use of a multimodal corpus that allows for the analyzation and comparison of three conflictive speech acts (compliments, refusals, and apologies). Through the recordings and transcriptions of native and non-native speakers, the Multimodal Corpus of Spanish Speech Acts (COR.E.M.A.H.) shows the differences in their strategies when faced with each speech act. In this chapter, we will also see how to use this advanced resource in different ways to teach pragmatics in a class of Spanish as a foreign language.

Keywords: language pedagogy, pragmatics, intercultural communication, multimodal corpus, non-verbal communication.

---

1. IES Abroad, Madrid, Spain; titavama@gmail.com

How to cite this chapter: Vacas Matos, M. (2018). Multimodal Corpus of Spanish Speech Acts: main features and potential pedagogical uses. In F. Rosell-Aguilar, T. Beaven, & M. Fuertes Gutiérrez (Eds), *Innovative language teaching and learning at university: integrating informal learning into formal language education* (pp. 89-97). Research-publishing.net. https://doi.org/10.14705/rpnet.2018.22.779

Chapter 10

## 1. Introduction

Starting with Bouton (1990, 1992, 1994), Kasper and Rose (1999), Rose and Kasper (2001), and Kasper (2001), linguists began to gather the benefits of the instruction of pragmatics in the Second Language (SL) classroom. In 2001, the Common European Framework of Reference for languages (CEFR) was published, including the pragmatic competence within the communicative competence, which increased the visibility of pragmatics in the field of second language acquisition. Hidden behind the subject of 'culture', pragmatics and its manifestations in every linguistic community remained a mystery for students trying to get to grips with the culture they were facing. It was not until 2003 that Bardovi-Harlig and Mahan-Taylor (2003) presented a book, written by teachers and for teachers, about teaching pragmatics in the foreign language classroom. Recently, research in teaching methodology has been developing new ways of bringing pragmatics to the classroom (Alcón Soler, 2005; Félix-Brasdefer, 2008; Kasper, 2001; Rose & Kasper, 2001; Tateyama, 2001; Louw, Derwing, & Abbott, 2010). However, until now, there has not been a resource that could show how native and non-native speakers behave pragmatically in a given situation. The COR.E.M.A.H. (Vacas Matos, 2017) is the first resource of its kind to provide these kinds of materials.

## 2. The corpus

Most foreign language students spend many years trying to excel at the grammar rules, vocabulary, and syntax of the language they are studying. They practice extraordinarily difficult pronunciations, study irregular verbs, and the use of tenses to be able to communicate effectively without committing a pragmatic failure. However, after their tremendous effort, they still sound foreign in pragmatic terms (Bardovi-Harlig et al., 1991; Bouton, 1990, 1992, 1994; Cohen, 1995; House, 1996; Kasper, 2001; Louw et al., 2010; Olshtain & Cohen, 1990). They are missing the key that opens real communication between native speakers: authentic, natural, and genuine native behaviors.

Research shows that pragmatics is acquired through the interaction with native speakers living in the target culture, amongst locals. Olshtain and Blum-Kulka (1985) found that immigrants in Jerusalem needed at least ten years of daily coexistence with locals to behave like native speakers of Hebrew just in terms of their acceptability of target speech act behavior. Nonetheless, most SL students are not immigrants according to the Instituto Cervantes (2016), and do not have the chance to live abroad for a long period of time to experience natural conversations with native speakers. This is how the idea of creating a multimodal video corpus of pragmatic behavior was conceived: to provide those students with informal native conversations they did not have access to.

More than 150 hours of role-play conversations of pairs of Americans (average age=20.7 for the intermediate group, and 29.79 for the advanced group) and pairs of Spaniards (average age=30.8) were recorded in order to have enough material to compose a substantial corpus. The total number of subjects of the corpus is 72: 24 native speakers, and 48 non-native speakers divided in two groups by level, B1 and C1 in the CEFR. The role-plays were recorded in pairs from each group. In the three groups, most of the participants were women. Every group had 24 participants: intermediate, 8 male and 16 female; advanced, 5 male and 19 female; and native speakers, 7 male and 17 female. Subjects were asked to perform ten situations with just general instructions about the situations and their roles (complimenter or receiver, for instance). In the end, three situations were chosen to configure the website corpus, given their conflictive intercultural outcomes, and because of their face-threatening nature: compliments, refusals of help, and apologies. One hundred and eight videos were transcribed and tagged for strategies, including non-verbal annotations, upgraders, and downgraders. This way, researchers, teachers, and students can access the version of the transcriptions they prefer to use:

- just the transcription of the role-play;

- the annotated transcription of the role-play (with the non-verbal language also transcribed); and

## Chapter 10

- the transcription with annotations and the strategies tagged, so they can see what the behavioral patterns of the individuals are for a given situation.

In addition to the video transcriptions, the corpus also has a search function (by word or strategy), which produces results that are clickable and that take the searcher to the exact role-play where the word or the strategy has appeared. Likewise, the strategies used in every tagged transcription are listed and clickable, so they can be easily located within the text.

Another feature of COR.E.M.A.H. is that the data from the subjects (age, gender, study of the language, and study abroad time, etc.), are visible and easily downloadable for every role-play, as Figure 1 shows.

Figure 1. View of one of the videos and transcriptions of the COR.E.M.A.H. webpage

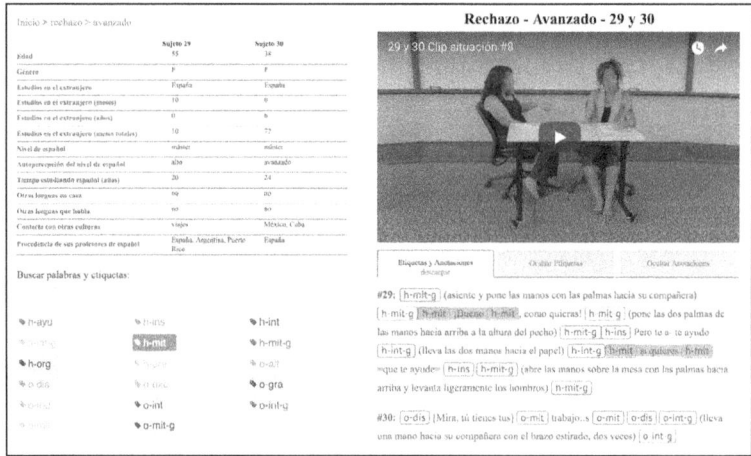

## 3. Results

This corpus was created to corroborate the hypothesis that advanced and intermediate learners would show similar behaviors in terms of pragmatics, and the hypothesis has been corroborated. The data shows that American students behave similarly amongst themselves, and in a different way than Spaniards do. Supporting the findings of several researchers (Alcón Soler, 2005; Bardovi-Harlig et al., 1991; Bouton, 1994; Félix-Brasdefer, 2008; House, 1996; House & Kasper, 1981; Kasper, 2001; Kasper & Rose, 1999; Louw et al., 2010; Olshtain & Cohen, 1990; Rose, 1994; Tateyama, 2001; Tateyama et al., 1997), the COR.E.M.A.H. reinforces the idea that pragmatics should be explicitly taught in order to be assimilated and, therefore, learned and acquired.

### 3.1. Analysis of the corpus data

The analysis of the data shows that the subjects with a higher level of proficiency in Spanish showed a similar level of pragmatic competence as those with an intermediate level. Even if the advanced subjects showed a higher level of lexical or grammatical competence, their pragmatic behavior was identical. However, it needs to be acknowledged that several subjects in both groups acted in a way that was more similar to Spaniards than to the way their classmates did. Not surprisingly, these subjects were the ones who spent more time abroad, and also, built up relationships of friendship or even love and family relationships with the locals. This fact reinforces the aim of the creation of COR.E.M.A.H. – performing speech acts in Spanish in order to provide students and teachers with different examples of native and non-native speakers.

### 3.2. Pedagogical uses

The use of *realia* or, in the case of COR.E.M.A.H., videos of real speakers producing natural speech acts is – if the students do not have the possibility of traveling abroad – one of the best ways to show how individuals behave in normal life (Cohen, 1995; Lorenzo-Dus, 2008), and how a learner can succeed in communication in ordinary contexts. This resource can be used in several ways by teachers, from just using the transcriptions of the videos (tagged and annotated, or not), to analyzing the non-verbal language, the movements, the proxemics, or even the tone of voice of the speakers. Some ideas of how the COR.E.M.A.H. can be used are the following:

- taking only the Spanish role-plays of the corpus to use the videos and transcriptions as models and play them in class as examples, analyzing them pragmatically in terms of communication to bring the informal conversations closer to the classroom;

- through the comparisons of performances of different individuals within the same group and different groups, studying their patterns and how they differ amongst each other upon the resolution of the three situations proposed;

- telling the students to role-play the situations before watching the videos (or watching the videos with the voice off) for further comparison and evaluation of strategies used amongst the students themselves and those used by native and non-native speakers in the corpus;

- using the transcriptions of the corpus, making the students perform them, and then afterwards showing the videos with the original communication produced by native speakers; and

- using the transcriptions to analyze the appearance in the recordings of discourse markers, upgraders, downgraders, constructions, expressions, interjections, etc.

## 4. Conclusion

Given the lack of multimodal resources, but specifically, resources created to learn the informal register and pragmatics of the language, COR.E.M.A.H. provides the foreign Spanish language class with natural language and conversations which are typically absent in the foreign language class and current manuals.

Results of analyzing the data in COR.E.M.A.H. showed that students need explicit instruction in order to succeed as intercultural speakers in these three complex speech acts. There are still many speech acts to record and transcribe, as well as different types of role-play pairs performing for COR.E.M.A.H., like intercultural pairs, or English learners acting out the role-plays in English, as well as native speakers of English. We encourage researchers and teachers to build more corpora and activities based on the idea of role-plays and natural behavior so that students have access to models of accurate pragmatic behavior to avoid pragmatic failure.

## References

Alcón Soler, E. (2005). Does instruction work for learning pragmatics in the EFL context? *System: An International Journal of Educational Technology and Applied Linguistics, 33*(3), 417-435.

Bardovi-Harlig, K., & Mahan-Taylor, R. (2003). *Teaching pragmatics*. United States Department of State.

Bardovi-Harlig, K., Hartford, B., Mahan-Taylor, R., Morgan, M., & Reynolds, D. (1991). Developing pragmatic awareness: closing the conversation. *ELT Journal, 45*(1), 4-15.

Bouton, L. F. (1990). The effective use of implicature in English: why and how it should be taught in the ESL classroom. In L. F. Bouton & Y. Kachru (Eds), *Pragmatics and language learning* (vol. 1) (pp. 43-51). University of Illinois: Division of English as an International Language.

Bouton, L. F. (1992). The interpretation of implicature in English by NNS: does it come automatically--without being explicitly taught? In L. F. Bouton & Y. Kachru (Eds), *Pragmatics and language learning* (vol. 3) (pp. 53-65). University of Illinois: Division of English as an International Language.

Bouton, L. (1994). Conversational implicature in a second language: learned slowly when not deliberately taught. *Journal of Pragmatics, 22*(2), 157-167. https://doi.org/10.1016/0378-2166(94)90065-5

Cohen, A. (1995). Investigating the production of speech act sets. In J. Neu & S. Gass (Eds), *Speech acts across cultures: challenges to communication in a second language. Studies on language acquisition*, 11 (pp. 21-43). Walter de Gruyter, Inc.

Félix-Brasdefer, J. (2008). Perceptions of refusals to invitations: exploring the minds of foreign language learners. *Language Awareness, 17*(3), 195-211. https://doi.org/10.1080/09658410802146818

House, J. (1996). Developing pragmatic fluency in English as a foreign language: routines and metapragmatic awareness. *Studies in Second Language Acquisition, 18*(2), 225-252. https://doi.org/10.1017/S0272263100014893

House, J., & Kasper, G. (1981). Politeness markers in English and German. In F. Columas (Ed.), *Conversational routine: explorations in standardized communication situations and prepatterned speech* (pp. 157-185). Mouton Publishers. https://doi.org/10.1515/9783110809145.157

Instituto Cervantes. (2016). El español: una lengua viva. Informe 2016. www.cervantes.es. http://www.cervantes.es/imagenes/File/prensa/EspanolLenguaViva16.pdf

Kasper, G. (2001). Classroom research on interlanguage pragmatics. In K. R. Rose & G. Kasper (Eds), *Pragmatics in language teaching* (pp. 33- 60). Cambridge University Press. https://doi.org/10.1017/CBO9781139524797.006

Kasper, G., & Rose, K. R. (1999). Pragmatics and SLA. *Annual Review of Applied Linguistics, 19*, 81-104. https://doi.org/10.1017/S0267190599190056

Lázaro Ruiz, H. (2014). *Las estrategias de respuesta al acto de habla del cumplido sobre apariencia y posesión en español peninsular y su tratamiento en los manuales de ele: estudio sociopragmático*. PhD. Universidad Antonio de Nebrija.

Lorenzo-Dus, N. (2008). Compliment responses among British and Spanish university students: a contrastive study. *Journal of Pragmatics, 33*(1), 107-127. https://doi.org/10.1016/S0378-2166(99)00127-7

Lörscher, W., & Rainer Schulze. (1988). On polite speaking and foreign language classroom discourse. *International Review of Applied Linguistics in Language Teaching, 26*(3), 183-199. https://doi.org/10.1515/iral.1988.26.3.183

Louw, K., Derwing, T., & Abbott, M. (2010). Teaching pragmatics to L2 learners for the workplace: the job interview. *Canadian Modern Language Review, 66*(5), 739-758. https://doi.org/10.3138/cmlr.66.5.739

Olshtain, E., & Blum-Kulka, S. (1985). Degree of approximation: nonnative reactions to native speech act behavior. In S. Gass & C. Madden (Eds), *Input in second language acquisition* (pp. 303-325). Newbury House.

Olshtain, E., & Cohen, A. (1990). The learning of complex speech act behavior. *TESL Canada Journal, 7*(2), 45-65. https://doi.org/10.18806/tesl.v7i2.568

Rose, K. (1994). Pragmatics consciousness-raising in an EFL context. In L. F. Bouton & Y. Kachru (Eds), *Pragmatics and language learning* (vol. 5) (pp. 52-63). University of Illinois: Division of English as an International Language.

Rose, K., & Kasper, G. (2001). *Pragmatics in language teaching.* Cambridge University Press. https://doi.org/10.1017/CBO9781139524797

Tateyama, Y. (2001). Explicit and implicit teaching of pragmatic routines: Japanese sumimasen. In K. Rose & G. Kasper (Eds), *Pragmatics in language teaching* (pp. 200-222). Cambridge University Press. https://doi.org/10.1017/CBO9781139524797.015

Tateyama, Y., Kasper, G., Mui, L., Tay, H., & Thananart, O. (1997). Explicit and implicit teaching of pragmatics routines. In L. F. Bouton (Ed.), *Pragmatics and language learning* (vol. 8) (pp.145-177). University of Illinois.

Vacas Matos, M. (2017). *COR.E.M.A.H. (Corpus Español Multimodal de Actos de Habla).* Coremah.com. http://www.coremah.com

# 11. Twitter as a formal and informal language learning tool: from potential to evidence

### Fernando Rosell-Aguilar[1]

## Abstract

Twitter[2] can be used as a language learning tool and this potential has been identified by a number of scholars. This chapter presents an overview of the identified potential of Twitter as a language learning tool and presents an overview of different studies carried out to provide evidence of language learning using Twitter in different contexts. It concludes that, although there is evidence of language acquisition in formal contexts, more research is needed to inform how Twitter is used in informal settings.

Keywords: Twitter, language learning, autonomous learning, social media, microblogging.

## 1. Introduction

Twitter is a multi-platform Social Networking Site (SNS) available to users from a range of devices, mobile or not. Users can post short messages (tweets) made up of up to 280 characters (the limit was 140 characters until November 2017). Twitter supports sharing photographs and video (including live streaming), hyperlinks to online resources, and creating short polls. Since Twitter was launched in 2006, the microblogging tool has gone from being a little-known service to a world-wide phenomenon with massive impact on news, politics,

---

1. The Open University, Milton Keynes, United Kingdom; fernando.rosell-aguilar@open.ac.uk

2. Twitter, Tweet, Retweet and the Twitter logo are trademarks of Twitter, Inc. or its affiliates.

**How to cite this chapter:** Rosell-Aguilar, F. (2018). Twitter as a formal and informal language learning tool: from potential to evidence. In F. Rosell-Aguilar, T. Beaven, & M. Fuertes Gutiérrez (Eds), *Innovative language teaching and learning at university: integrating informal learning into formal language education* (pp. 99-106). Research-publishing.net. https://doi.org/10.14705/rpnet.2018.22.780

business, entertainment, sports, and education among many other fields. By 2017, Twitter had 330 million monthly active users, with 80% of users accessing the tool from mobile devices (Twitter, 2017). Users utilise hashtags to make the topics of their tweets more visible and searchable, and Twitter lists the most popular issues being discussed as trending topics, with geographical variations to reflect different issues around the world.

Due to affordances such as hosting media-rich resources, and private and public communication, Twitter, like other SNSs such as Facebook, can be used as a medium for both formal and informal learning. In this chapter, formal learning is defined as learning directed by an educator in a formal setting, such as a school or university, and informal learning as learning that is self-directed by the learner, who takes charge of the initiatives and activities they undertake towards learning (also referred to as self-directed learning and autonomous learning). It has been acknowledged that "informal education plays a key role for language learning" (European Commission, 2012, p. 16), and this chapter will evaluate the potential of Twitter for language learning and the evidence found so far to support whether that potential is being realised.

## 2. Twitter and language learning

In the early days of Twitter, English was the dominant language used in this platform. In 2006, 98% of tweets were written in English (GNIP, 2014). Seven years later, although still the most used language on Twitter, the proportion of tweets in English had fallen to 51%, followed by Japanese (14.8%), Spanish (13.4%), Portuguese (5.1%), Indonesian (3.2%), Arabic (3.2%), French (2.4%), Turkish (1.8%), Russian (1.3%), and Korean (1.1%) (GNIP, 2014). Twitter currently supports 40 different languages (Twitter, 2017) and also offers a translation tool that identifies the language of the tweet and translates it to the default language of the user's account.

The 140-character limit that characterised tweets for its first decade was seen as both an advantage and a hindrance. While some detractors felt that it stopped the natural flow of language and could lead to the use of bad grammar (Grosseck & Holotescu, 2008), other authors claimed that the limit encouraged more precise thinking, editing, and synthesising of language (Dunlap & Lowenthal, 2009; Plutino, 2017). The language used to tweet is determinant of how restrictive the character limit is: whereas in some languages this limited the message to just a few words, in other languages such as Chinese or Japanese, 140 characters allow for much more content to be expressed, most likely the reason why the limit remains at 140 characters for languages such as Chinese, Japanese, and Korean, even after November 2017.

Many authors have highlighted the potential of Twitter in particular as a tool for language learning (Borau, Ullrich, Feng, & Shen, 2009; Dickens, 2008; Harmandaoglu, 2012; Newgarden, 2009). Craig (2012) differentiated between linguistic benefits (noticing vocabulary, expressions, idioms, and grammar), cultural benefits (access to native speakers and insight into their routines, opinions, media, and general interests), and social benefits (extending learning outside the classroom, social presence, and distribution). Borau et al. (2009) proposed that on Twitter, language learners can access exposure to the target language and also learn to express their thoughts in the target language. In contrast, Newgarden (2009) focussed instead on engagement and participation in communities of language users.

Other benefits for language learning include opportunities to learn about current affairs, politics, or culture (Reinhardt, Wheeler, & Ebner, 2010), engaging in language play (Hattem, 2014), posting homework and brief questions to respond to, and intercultural information and exchanges (Lee & Markey, 2014). In addition, Twitter can help raise awareness of popular culture, and be used to share experiences of visiting a target language area (Plutino, 2017).

Figure 1 presents an overview of the different potential uses of Twitter as a language learning tool, some of which overlap. Although Twitter is primarily a written medium, the ability to livestream video and link to audio and video resources (self-produced or content from others), means that interaction is not limited to text.

Figure 1. Potential uses of Twitter as a language learning tool

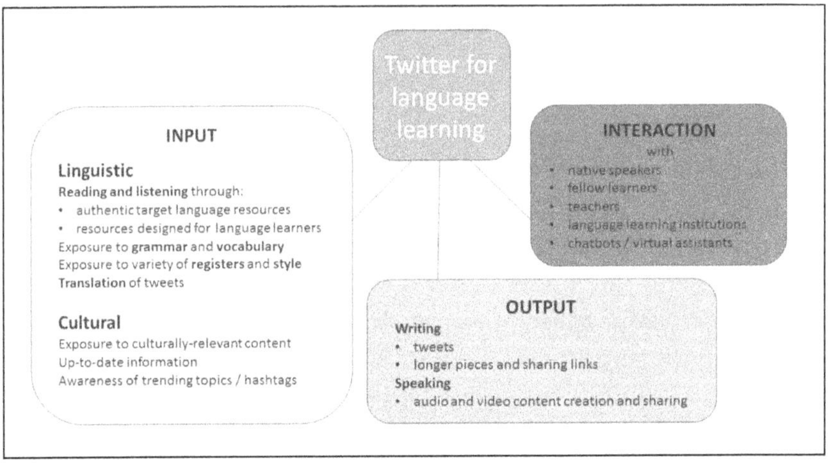

```
                    Twitter for
                    language
        INPUT       learning          INTERACTION
                                           with
Linguistic                          • native speakers
Reading and listening through:      • fellow learners
 • authentic target language resources  • teachers
 • resources designed for language learners  • language learning institutions
Exposure to grammar and vocabulary   • chatbots / virtual assistants
Exposure to variety of registers and style
Translation of tweets
                              OUTPUT
Cultural                  Writing
Exposure to culturally-relevant content  • tweets
Up-to-date information     • longer pieces and sharing links
Awareness of trending topics / hashtags  Speaking
                           • audio and video content creation and sharing
```

The types of uses presented in Figure 1 can be part of teacher-directed activities in a formal learning environment, in or outside the classroom, or can be undertaken by learners in an informal manner as self-directed activities. Doing the latter allows language learning activities to be learner-centred, as they can choose who to follow and what topics to focus on depending on their own interests.

## 3. Evidence of engagement and learning

A number of studies have looked into the use of Twitter for a variety of areas of language learning. Some of the research has focussed on interaction among students and also with native speakers: Ullrich et al. (2008) carried out one of the earliest studies into the use of Twitter for language learning with very positive results: 94% of their students, based in China, believed that their English had improved with the help of Twitter. The students communicated with each other in English through Twitter and half of them also communicated with native speakers. Similar results were found by Kim, Park, and Baek (2011): from their study of 45 Korean school children learning English as a Foreign Language (EFL), they concluded that the use of Twitter had stimulated their mixed-ability participants to produce output in the target language and engage in social interaction with fellow students as well as native speakers. Similarly, Antenos-Conforti (2009) analysed the tweets that 22 of his students of intermediate Italian tweeted, as well as the data from a survey into their experience of using Twitter. He concluded that the introduction of Twitter into his course helped the students develop a sense of community and encouraged participation, creating a virtual extension of his classroom. In contrast, Craig (2012) used Twitter over three semesters in 2010-11 for an advanced EFL writing class in Korea. Students were required to tweet daily and provide feedback on others' writing. Although students' knowledge of the tool improved, their engagement was very teacher-directed and the results disappointing; he eventually abandoned its use in class.

Jiménez-Muñoz (2014) looked into the use of Twitter to promote communication among students and tutor/students, engage students in target language use, and get involved in a more sophisticated use of the language, as well as error correction. He found an increase in both the quantity and quality of interactions in the target language among his students. In one of the few research projects focussing on the use of Twitter to teach pronunciation, Mompean and Fouz-González (2016) set up a series of tweets for their participants (16 Spanish EFL students). The tweets highlighted commonly-occurring errors in pronunciation for Spanish speakers: silent letters, unusual grapheme-phoneme correspondences, and misplaced lexical stress. Correct pronunciation was highlighted either within the text of the tweets or with links to audio and video resources. The researchers found high levels of interaction with the tweets. All participants who took part in both pre- and post-pronunciation tests showed significant improvement. Other attempts to encourage learners to improve their pronunciation using Twitter include the project by Plutino (2017), who encouraged her students to use the speech-to-text feature on their mobile phones to compose tweets in Italian. Although using this method slowed down the process of tweeting, 75% of the participants in her study found the process helpful to self-assess their performance and identify pronunciation and accuracy errors.

Other Twitter studies have focussed on intercultural exchanges as well as language learning. Lomicka and Lord (2012) carried out a study with 13 US students of

French and 12 French students of English using Twitter to build a community and language practice outside of class time. Their data suggested that the participants quickly formed a collaborative community that enabled them to learn, share, and reflect. The students reported that they had learnt more about French culture than in previous courses, gained confidence, improved their reading skills, and learnt from each other's tweets. They also indicated that they were more likely to use Twitter again for learning. Similarly, Lee and Markey (2014) carried out an intercultural exchange project between ten students of advanced Spanish in the US and 18 students of advanced English in Spain utilising a number of Web 2.0 tools. Twitter was used to make connections among participants, establish good rapports and build group dynamics, exchange personal interests, academic work, and cultural perspectives, and brainstorm ideas and make arrangements for assignments. The researchers found very positive perceptions of Twitter for these purposes and in particular for building community and interpersonal relationships, but some students felt limited by the 140-character length and message order, and one student was very reluctant to use Twitter.

Whilst the research studies presented have found some evidence of engagement with language learning activity and increases in confidence, community development, and language acquisition, most research into the use of Twitter for language learning has been based on activities that were teacher-directed. In many cases, participation was compulsory and in some of the studies learners had to create Twitter accounts for the purposes of the research. Whilst the data these studies show remains of interest, the evidence presented does not capture the more natural type of activities learners engage in of their own accord. Evidence of self-directed interaction and engagement with language learners and resources can often be found in the Twitter accounts of language learners, many of whom engage with language learning accounts such as those from language institutions such as The British Council, Alliance Française, or the Goethe Institute, for example. Some learners tweet in their target language and share news from the areas where their target language is spoken, as well as recommendations for resources and language learning tips. However, there is a dearth of research into informal language learning through Twitter, and that is an area worthy of further research.

## 4. Conclusion

The recent doubling of the character count from 140 to 280 is likely to have an effect on the way users express themselves. It may reduce the number of acronyms and abbreviations used as well as the number of instances of 'bad' grammar (skipping articles or prepositions, for example). It may also lead to more reflection and less concise posts, thus addressing the concerns some researchers had expressed regarding the 140-character limit (Grosseck & Holotescu, 2008). The changes to the way Twitter users express themselves after the move from 140 to 280 characters will be an interesting area for further investigation.

Although this chapter has focussed on the learner experience of using Twitter for language learning purposes, it is worth mentioning that language teachers also engage in the sharing of resources and experiences through hashtags such as #Langchat and #MFLtwitterati, which are examples of teachers seeking and supporting each other for continuous professional development through Twitter.

## References

Antenos-Conforti, E. (2009). Microblogging on Twitter: social networking in intermediate Italian classes. In L. Lomicka & G. Lord (Eds), *The next generation: social networking and online collaboration in foreign language learning* (pp. 59-90). CALICO.

Borau, K., Ullrich, C., Feng, J., & Shen, R. (2009). Microblogging for language learning: using twitter to train communicative and cultural competence. In *Advances in Web Based Learning–ICWL 2009* (pp. 78-87). Springer. https://doi.org/10.1007/978-3-642-03426-8_10

Craig, D. (2012, September 6). *Twitter for academic writing* [Blog post]. http://www.danielcraig.com/2012/09/06/twitter-for-academic-writing-2/

Dickens, S. (2008, April 29). *Twitter – microblogging* [Blog post]. Digitalang. http://www.digitalang.com/2008/04/twitter-microblogging/

Dunlap, J. C., & Lowenthal, P. R. (2009).Tweeting the night away: using Twitter to enhance social presence. *Journal of Information Systems Education, 20*(2), 129-135.

European Commission. (2012). *Commission staff working document - Language competencies for employability, mobility and growth.* http://ec.europa.eu/education/news/rethinking/sw372_en.pdf

GNIP. (2014). *Twitter languages*. https://gnip.com/blank/twitter-language-viz/

Grosseck, G., & Holotescu, C. (2008, April). *Can we use Twitter for educational activities*. In 4th international scientific conference, eLearning and software for education, Bucharest, Romania.

Harmandaoglu, E. (2012). *The use of Twitter in language learning and teaching.* Paper presented at the International Conference "ICT for Language Learning" 5th Edition, Florence.

Hattem, D. (2014). Microblogging activities: language play and tool transformation. *Language Learning & Technology, 18*(2), 151-174.

Jiménez-Muñoz, A. (2014). *Quantity and quality: using Twitter in the ESP classroom*. Paper presented at the TISLID'14 - Second International Workshop on Technological Innovation for Specialized Linguistic Domains: Lifelong Learning on the Move Conference, Ávila, Spain, 7-9 May, 2014.

Kim, E.-Y., Park, S.-M., & Baek, S.-H. (2011). Twitter and implications for its use in EFL learning. *Multimedia-Assisted Language Learning, 14*(2), 113-137.

Lee, L., & Markey, A. (2014). A study of learners' perceptions of online intercultural exchange through Web 2.0 technologies. *ReCALL, 26*(3), 281-297. https://doi.org/10.1017/S0958344014000111

Lomicka, L., & Lord, G. (2012). A tale of tweets: analyzing microblogging among language learners. *System, 40(1)*, 48-63. https://doi.org/10.1016/j.system.2011.11.001

Mompean, J. A., & Fouz-González, J. (2016). Twitter-based EFL pronunciation instruction. *Language Learning & Technology, 20*(1), 166–190.

Newgarden, K. (2009). Twitter. *The Electronic Journal for English as a Second Language (TESL-EJ), 13*(2), 761-779.

Plutino, A. (2017). Teachers as awakeners: a collaborative approach in language learning and social media. In C. Álvarez-Mayo, A. Gallagher-Brett, & F. Michel (Eds), *Innovative language teaching and learning at university: enhancing employability* (pp. 115-125). Research-publishing.net. https://doi.org/10.14705/rpnet.2017.innoconf2016.661

Reinhardt, W., Wheeler, S., & Ebner, M. (2010). All I need to know about twitter in education I learned in kindergarten. In *Key Competencies in the Knowledge Society* (pp. 322-332). Springer. https://doi.org/10.1007/978-3-642-15378-5_31

Twitter. (2017). https://about.twitter.com/company

Ullrich, C., Borau, K., Luo, H., Tan, X., Shen, L., & Shen, R. (2008, April). Why web 2.0 is good for learning and for research: principles and prototypes. In *Proceedings of the 17th international conference on World Wide Web* (pp. 705-714). ACM. https://doi.org/10.1145/1367497.1367593

# Section 3.

# The polyglot community: an interview with Richard Simcott

# 12. The polyglot community: an interview with Richard Simcott, by Tita Beaven

## Tita Beaven[1] and Richard Simcott[2]

---

The closing plenary session at the InnoConf17 conference was an informal interview that Tita Beaven conducted with Richard Simcott, which we reproduce here in an edited version.

**TB[3]**: So, Richard, you are a polyglot. What is that?

**RS[4]**: Well, I suppose polyglot will take you back to the Greek: 'poly' is a lot and 'glot' is languages or tongues. So, someone who speaks lots of languages. How many that is is up for debate and a lot of research.

**TB**: Ok, so we know what polyglot means, but what is a polyglot for you?

**RS**: I think for me a polyglot really is somebody who sets out intentionally to learn multiple languages, say more than maybe just your school language that you carry on studying because you like the culture or fall in love with it… I'm not sure whether to use the word serial, but a 'serial language learner'. So, I guess it's about doing something that you don't necessarily need for your education, you don't necessarily need for your work; you're learning languages just because you want to…

---

1. The Open University, Milton Keynes, United Kingdom; tita.beaven@open.ac.uk

2. Polyglot Conference, Skopje, Republic of Macedonia; richard_simcott@hotmail.com

3. Tita Beaven, interviewer

4. Richard Simcott, interviewee

**How to cite this chapter:** Beaven, T., & Simcott, R. (2018). The polyglot community: an interview with Richard Simcott, by Tita Beaven. In F. Rosell-Aguilar, T. Beaven, & M. Fuertes Gutiérrez (Eds), *Innovative language teaching and learning at university: integrating informal learning into formal language education* (pp. 109-118). Research-publishing.net. https://doi.org/10.14705/rpnet.2018.22.781

---

© 2018 Tita Beaven and Richard Simcott (CC BY)

# Chapter 12

**TB:** But you did study languages yourself. Tell us a little bit about where it all started.

**RS:** I grew up in Chester, around the border of England and Wales, and so around me, there were lots of very interesting accents. I heard other languages around me; Welsh, Thai, because my stepmom is from Thailand, and I was studying languages at school, picking up books, and listening to kids speaking languages on holidays and so on. That's what sparked my interest. I was also studying languages in a formal environment at school and then at university. My university course at the University of Hull was a BA [Bachelor of Arts] programme in combined languages, and they allowed me to do French, Spanish, and Italian, with Portuguese as a subsidiary language. But then they said that if I wanted I could sit on another degree, so I started the Scandinavian studies degree as well, and did Icelandic and Swedish. And then decided I could also study languages by myself as well, so I am a bit of serial language learner!

**TB:** Okay, so you started learning languages formally and then you've carried on studying languages informally. What's the difference?

**RS:** The difference I think is that in formal language learning, at university, for instance, there are these criteria that you need to meet, and it can become a bit like a tick box exercise. Sometimes those box-ticking activities can diminish your motivation… But I do think it's really important for people to study in an academic way, to understand that language learning has to be rigorous to some degree, depending on what you want it for of course, but, when I was learning on my own, I could go off and do my own thing and meander through the languages and pick up as much or as little as I wanted, and I wasn't constrained by these box-ticking activities that I had at university. But I enjoyed both…

**TB:** And can I ask you then, how do you use your languages now, especially at work?

**RS:** I work for a social media management agency called the Social Element. I am their languages director, so I give advice on multilingual projects for our clients who have projects for their various campaigns and products on social media (Facebook, Twitter, YouTube, etc.). I am responsible for quality assurance. So, when we are producing materials in different languages for a specific campaign, I am the point of reference in the company to check the material and to understand the feedback from clients. I also project manage, working out how to use our teams and our resources to the best of our abilities.

**TB:** And I know that you also use languages at home, so tell us about the languages you use in that context.

**RS:** I am married to a Macedonian and we live now in the Republic of Macedonia, in the capital, Skopje. At home, my wife and I only speak Macedonian amongst us. My daughter is ten, and she speaks Macedonian and English. She was born in the UK and I spoke to her in French from birth, so she also speaks French; she did her nursery school in French and now she studies in English at school, where she also does French and Macedonian as her first languages. From the age of 16 months I also introduced Spanish and German. So, she has five home languages, which are the languages we use at home on a daily basis, and then she also understands some others like Bulgarian, Serbian, and Italian.

**TB:** How do you manage? For those of us who are from bilingual families, bringing up a kid bilingually is hard enough, so how do you manage five languages?

**RS:** Good time management is all I can say! It was quite easy to do French and English from birth because she couldn't say anything back, so I just said the same thing twice in the two languages. So, if I sang a lullaby in French, then I'd sing either a similar one or the same one in English and vice versa. I was able to really give her exactly equal doses of both languages until she could speak. Because we were living in the UK at the time, I then switched to only speaking French with her because her input from outside groups and other family members and friends was English, so I could switch quite comfortably to just French at home to make it a lot easier. My wife just spoke Macedonian to her, and my wife and I spoke Macedonian to each other. Until she was three, my daughter only spoke

## Chapter 12

to me in Macedonian – she would say bits and bobs in other languages, but she would use Macedonian mostly. I think it's because she thought that: 'as mum speaks to dad in that language, I speak to dad in that language'.

And there was a turning point at that age where we thought that she was doing so well with the three languages… She was saying three-word sentences by the age one, so doing well compared to a monolingual child. Therefore we decided that maybe she was able to pick up languages easily and we decided to introduce another language, but we couldn't decide between German or Spanish. I spent time playing with her every day and I decided to just use both. I would play with her for an hour in German and an hour in Spanish, and she seemed to like them both and pick them both up. And within a couple of months she was using words and preferring words in those languages over the other three, so we just carried on with both till this day.

**TB:** And she's happy to do it? She hasn't rebelled?

**RS:** No, she hasn't. She did say to me once when she was three: 'Daddy, why do you speak to me in Spanish?' And I said: 'Because a lot of people don't know how to speak in Spanish. When you go to school when you are older, you'll probably have to study Spanish anyway, and this way you're going to know more than the other kids and you'll have a head start'. And she just said: 'Clever Daddy!'.

**TB:** Indeed! But going back to the polyglot community, how did that start?

**RS:** Well, like probably many people here, when you are growing up, you like languages and you don't really have anyone to communicate that ambition, love, and drive with and I felt the same way, and all the way through school and even at university, I expected to find people like me, but I really found very few people who actually had the same real passion that I have for languages. As I got a bit older and the internet started developing and people started speaking in online forums, I got involved in a few online forums. There was one called 'How to learn any language' or something like that, and I was on that forum for a couple of years, about ten years ago. I noticed that more and more people were joining, and I made a video on YouTube speaking in 16 of the languages I'd studied at that point. They were at different levels because I wanted to show that there's some I spoke really well and others not so fluently. My idea was to reach out to like-minded people and also to show other people in the world who are in the same position that I was that they are not alone; and it's kind of a party trick... everyone who knew me in real life always wanted me to do this party trick. They would wheel me in and say: 'This is the one who speaks all these languages! Go on, say something in every language!'. So, I thought this video would serve all of these purposes in one go. I made the video and from there, I started meeting people who shared this passion. I started making real connections with real-life people, and we started meeting in person, even in one-on-one situations. One summer in Poland, I was talking to one of my friends and a few people noticed me on the streets, and they approached me because they had seen my videos; and that got me thinking...

So, that's how the idea of putting together a polyglot conference came about. The name of the Polyglot Conference came out of the fact that there was beginning to be a polyglot community online. I decided that the scope of the polyglot conference was going to be to unite academia with people working in languages from very different circles: translation, teaching, business, anything, and then just language learners who love languages and to bring them all together under one roof.

I wanted the expertise from the academic world because the injection of that knowledge is super important to feed the conference, and I also wanted to generate conversations and to get people asking questions and to see how the practicalities of academic work and academic research can be used in other fields that maybe we've not even thought about before, and that cross-pollination I saw is very, very important. For the first Polyglot Conference I picked Budapest for a couple of reasons: one was that it was a homage to Kató Lomb, a famous Hungarian polyglot. The second reason was a bit of an ironic one, as very few people learn Hungarian as a foreign language. So, in 2013, I rented a theatre in the center of Budapest and managed to get

140 people there over a weekend. I was on stage for 20 hours introducing all of these people I'd met from all corners of the globe... they came from America, all over Europe, Asia, you name it!

From there, actually, quite a lot of things happened. People who had been talking online got together in real life, and quite a few things were born out of it. One was the Polyglot Gathering, which is another event. Judith Meyer, a woman I had met on the polyglot forums online, came up to me and said: 'do you mind me doing something similar to this in Berlin next year? An event more laid back, inspired by the events run by the Esperanto community, where people can get together and talk about language learning and practise their languages?'. So the Polyglot Gathering grew out of the Polyglot Conference; it started in 2014 and has been taking place every year since. Then the Add1Challenge grew out from one of the presentations at the conference. The Add1Challenge is basically an online community where people set to learn a language for three months, and they make videos and document their learning as they go, using iTalki tutors, using course books... and they may be studying the language in a formal context as well. They document their progression in the language and it serves as motivation for them. All these great things came out of that initial meeting in Budapest. Benny Lewis, another well-known polyglot, came and presented at the conference, and he's now written some Teach Yourself courses... Some really interesting things just came out of this first conference, and we are now planning the fifth Polyglot Conference in Reykjavik. So we went from Budapest, where we had 140 attendees to, Novi Sad, where we've worked with the Serbian government, who liked the idea of the conference and supported us, where we had 240 attendees. The next event was in New York, where 420 people came to Manhattan. Now we're able to get sponsorship and interest, so in Greece, in 2016, it was just absolutely out of this world: roughly 450 people came to the conference. And this year it's in Iceland[5]. Every year, we celebrate the local languages and the local cultures. Every year we also try to find a theme, so in Reykjavik, one of the themes is autism and multilingualism. There is a lot of interesting research into the

---

5. The Polyglot Conference in Reykjavik took place in October 2017, and attracted 400 attendees. The next Polyglot Conference will take place in October 2018 in Ljubljana.

autistic spectrum and language learning. We've noticed in the community a lot of people identify on that spectrum and are very accomplished language learners, so we wanted to salute that. Another theme of the conference was how technology can support minority languages.

**TB:** These events, both the conference and the gathering, are really interesting because they bring together language learners, rather than language teachers. I think the language learning and teaching landscape in the UK can be a bit grim, and yet these polyglot events are incredibly vibrant, they attract a lot of young learners who are passionate about languages. One of the things that I find refreshing and stimulating about the polyglot events is that, as a language teacher, it is great to be surrounded by expert language learners and it's like turning the tables on what we normally do. It's normally the expert teachers who tell the students what to learn and how to learn it, and this is the other way around. And it's fascinating in terms of the relationship between formal and informal learning. From your experience, what do you think these expert language learners can teach expert language teachers?

**RS:** I think that one of the key messages is that there are many different methods and there's not one magic pill that anyone can take to learn a language. I think that's one of the misconceptions. And also that the level of confidence of people signing up to learn languages is really low. You hear so often just in daily speech 'I'm terrible at learning languages, I can't learn languages, I always fail'… And of course it's not true, we know it's not true! It's just the lack of confidence and it's possibly because they haven't found the right way of learning a language for them, and the right things that stimulate and motivate them. These are the kinds of things that we hear at the conferences and at the gatherings. All these things are really helping to promote language learning to ordinary people, to really get that message to as many people as possible. I think that's the real key thing. Although the conference and the gathering grew from the polyglot community, they are for anyone interested in languages. There are people who are learning their first language and they come to one of these events that they say: 'Oh, I also want to learn this one now, and this one, and this one too'. They go and they come back energised and enthused.

Chapter 12

**TB:** Yes, I've found it is an amazingly welcoming community. It's really not about counting how many languages someone speaks, it's about sharing the fun and the love and the enjoyment of learning languages. The other thing I was going to ask you is that technology has played a central part in all of this, making all of this possible, from you posting your first video online to what the polyglot community has grown into; so how do polyglots use technology?

**RS:** All the time and every day! So, for instance, Skype and talking to teachers in different countries has become just an integral part of the daily or weekly routine of most people in the language community online. I certainly use it for any language projects, whether it's a short-term or a long-term language project I'm involved in. Because I'm living in the centre of Skopje, I don't hear that many Norwegians around me... So, when I was studying Norwegian, I found somebody to speak with online, and just met up regularly for a chat. There are also lots of people interacting together on social media, on Facebook groups, and on Twitter... But there are also lots of language apps, so you see more and more people signing up for Duolingo, Memrise, Babbel and the like, and using also the more interactive elements to well-known publishers such as Teach Yourself or Assimil...

**TB:** What about language exchanges? It is something we use a lot in formal contexts at university, but a lot of polyglots also do them regularly. Is it something that you use yourself, and what makes a good language exchange?

**RS:** Yes, and it works really well when you find someone you can really get on with. The same goes for teachers online. For instance, last year I was studying Greek and I found a great Greek teacher. We got on really well and I ended up going to his wedding in January with the whole family. I think when you meet somebody online and the chemistry's right, it works really well. Sometimes you need to go through a couple of people and find someone you gel with. What I find is having a clear idea in your head of what you want to achieve in the language is really important. It's good for the teacher to have a plan and to be structured if that's what you need. For example, I was learning Norwegian for a couple of months and my teacher said that as I already spoke Swedish and I could already understand her, we could just go straight to listening to podcasts and chat about them. And I said: 'You know what? No, I don't want to do that. I want to start from the beginning and make sure I've got all the basic vocabulary', because that's where the differences tend to be in some of these similar languages. I just took the Teach Yourself Norwegian book and went through each chapter with my teacher. So I would tell her what happened in the dialogue of the chapter, and tell her how that was relevant to my life. I changed the examples so it fitted with me, so I could talk about my life. It is important to be able to talk about what is relevant to your own life, because that's what you're going to use and I think when learners understand what language they need to have and what language is appropriate for their lives, that's when they get that buzz, that feeling, and that endorphin rush and think: 'Oh! This is actually useful! It's not just me learning random words and vocabulary that I can only use in obscure situations'. It also applies to students who are going on an Erasmus exchange, for instance. If you are going to spend some time in France, or in China, or whatever, what language do you need to learn that is going to be relevant to that setting?

**TB:** So it is important to make your learning relevant?

**RS:** Yes, make it personal.

**TB:** And take control… Speaking of the year abroad, the Erasmus programme is celebrating its 30$^{th}$ birthday. I remember when I went on my year abroad 30 years ago, we just went and that was that. Maybe once a month or so we would phone home, but we had no contact to speak of with our friends back home. Now, this has completely changed of course…

**RS:** I had the same experience as you. I went away and I was off the radar. I wasn't really in touch with anyone back home, I had to make new friends, and go out and do things that normal people do. Nowadays, it's quite different. I was working with a student who's just graduated from Cambridge and he was abroad in Germany, but he was getting these cheap flights every other weekend, going back home or going to see friends in other countries on their Erasmus exchange programmes. When I did my year abroad, for me to get home was really expensive back then, and even to call home was really expensive also.

Now you've got the internet, you've got Whatsapp, you've got all of these great things on your mobile phone and you can just be talking to someone anywhere else in the world. That was unthinkable then, and I do wonder how much people who go on a year abroad can immerse themselves in their target language and culture.

**TB:** So in fact, all those apps and resources that help language learners immerse themselves in the language and the culture they are studying also work the other way, and prevent students on their year abroad from fully immersing in the language and culture of the country they are visiting, because they are able to keep in touch so easily with their friends back home, and with TV, the news, and so on, online. One final question, Richard. How do you pick what language to study next?

**RS:** They pick me! Normally, if I've got plans to go somewhere then I might take on a language project: last year I went to the Polyglot Gathering in Bratislava, so I took on Slovak. I did this Slovak language challenge and gave a presentation in Slovak, which is a lot of fun. I'm going to Indonesia on Sunday for a month, so I'm learning Indonesian.

**TB:** Well, good luck with that, and thank you very much for sharing some of your knowledge and expertise with us.

**RS:** Thank you!

# Author index

**B**
Bárkányi, Zsuzsanna viii, 4, 9
Beaven, Tita vii, xiii, 1, 5, 109
Brick, Billy viii, 4, 49

**C**
Cervi-Wilson, Tiziana viii, 4, 49
Chen, Zhiqiong viii, 5, 67

**F**
Fuertes Gutiérrez, Mara vii, xiii, 1

**M**
Martínez-Carrasco, Robert ix, 4, 17
Mericka, Kirsten ix, 4, 59

**R**
Rosell-Aguilar, Fernando vii, xiii, 1, 5, 99

**S**
Salin, Sandra ix, 5, 79
Saona-Vallejos, Miguel Ángel ix, 4, 27
Simcott, Richard x, 5, 109

**V**
Vacas Matos, Marta x, 5, 89

**W**
Wang, Liang x, 4, 37

www.ingramcontent.com/pod-product-compliance
Lightning Source LLC
Chambersburg PA
CBHW031634160426
43196CB00006B/406